REVOLUTIONARY CHRISTIANITY

Revolutionary Christianity

THE 1966 SOUTH AMERICAN LECTURES

JOHN HOWARD YODER

EDITED BY
Paul Martens, Mark Thiessen Nation,
Matthew Porter, and Myles Werntz

 CASCADE *Books* · Eugene, Oregon

REVOLUTIONARY CHRISTIANITY
The 1966 South American Lectures

Cascade Books
An Imprint of Wipf and Stock Publishers
199 W. 8th Ave., Suite 3
Eugene, OR 97401

www.wipfandstock.com

ISBN: 13: 978-1-61097-000-6

Excerpts from Hendrik Berkhof, *Christ and the Powers*, trans. John Howard Yoder (Scottdale, PA: Herald Press, 1977) in chapter 11 used with permission.

Herald Press has also graciously granted permission to publish the following which include portions of previously published material:

1. Chapter 5—"Discipleship in the Sermon on the Mount" ("The Political Axioms of the Sermon on the Mount," *The Original Revolution: Essays on Christian Pacifism*, Scottdale, PA: Herald Press, 1971);

2. Chapter 9—"The Biblical View of History" and Chapter 12—"Constantinianism Old and New" ("Christ, The Hope of the World," *The Original Revolution*);

3. Chapter 10—"The Otherness of the Church," ("The Otherness of the Church," *The Royal Priesthood: Essays Ecclesiological and Ecumenical*, Scottdale, PA: Herald Press, 1994).

Cataloging-in-Publication data:

Yoder, John Howard.

Revolutionary Christianity : the 1966 South American lectures / John Howard Yoder ; edited by Paul Martens, Mark Thiessen Nation, Matthew Porter, and Myles Werntz.

xvi + 178 p. ; 23 cm.—Includes indexes.

ISBN: 13: 978-1-61097-000-6

1. Christian ethics—Mennonite authors—Addresses, essays, lectures. 2. Social ethics—Addresses, essays, lectures. I. Martens, Paul. II. Nation, Mark Thiessen. III. Porter, Matthew. IV. Werntz, Myles. V. Title.

BJ1251 Y7 2012

Manufactured in the U.S.A.

*There is no greater contribution that can be made by the tiny people of God
in the revolution of our age than to be that people,
both separate from the world and identified with its needs,
both the soul of society (without which it cannot live)
and its conscience (with which it cannot be at peace).*

—JOHN HOWARD YODER

Table of Contents

Introduction

IN HIS "PREFACE" TO *The Original Revolution*, published in 1971, John Howard Yoder sought to distance his work from the "faddist approach to theology" that dominated the late sixties, the approach that yielded "an enormous proliferation of interest and imagery around the concern of Christians for social change."[1] Slightly sarcastically, he noted: "A new book dealing with 'the revolution in theology' or 'theology for the revolution,' with politicking as a theological concern or with theology as a political event appeared almost every week."[2] Four and a half decades later, we are happy to introduce Yoder's very accessible subversive contribution to this late sixties proliferation of books on Christianity and revolution.

In 1966, the thirty-eight year old Yoder was invited to offer a series of summer lectures at the Seminario Evangelico Menonita in Montevideo, Uruguay, and the Facultad de Teológia Evangélica and the Seminario Internacional Teológico Bautista in Buenos Aires, Argentina.[3] The lectures that are gathered in this volume are part of the lasting legacy of Yoder's trip to South America, the written legacy that Yoder subsequently arranged, titled, and then left largely unpublished. It is our hope that the reader will come to see that these lectures may yet be as relevant today as they were when they would have been considered rather "faddish."

1. John Howard Yoder, *The Original Revolution: Essays on Christian Pacifism* (Scottdale, PA: Herald, 1971) 8.

2. Ibid.

3. Most of the particulars regarding Yoder's trip in the summer of 1966 come from: Yoder, "Report on South America Trip 22 May–8 July, 1966, 'Memo to Executive and Overseas Offices, MBMC,' July 25, 1966," Archives of the Mennonite Church, Hist. MSS 1–48, Box 32, file 13.

Historical Considerations

By 1966, Yoder was becoming well known in Mennonite circles as someone who was broadly educated, ecumenically experienced, and of significant intellectual stature.[4] Although he did not know much about Latin
America when the invitation was received, he had traveled extensively
in Europe since he first left for France in April, 1949, on an assignment
with Mennonite Central Committee; although he did not know Spanish,
he apparently added Spanish to his language repertoire (which included
French, German, and some Dutch at the time) through a program offered on cassette tapes;[5] although he did not know many South American
theologians, his extensive experience in ecumenical dialogue in Europe
(especially around issues related to pacifism and the free church) provided him with the tools necessary to navigate the exciting and challenging
theologies and communities he encountered in South America. Further,
by 1966, Yoder had six years of experience as an administrative assistant
with the Mennonite Board of Missions and Charities in Elkhart, Indiana.[6]

Yoder's trip to South America was not very long—May 22 to July
8—but the schedule was full. The two series of invited lectures served as
the foundation for the trip. It appears that he presented the series of lectures gathered as "The Believers Church" in both Montevideo and Buenos
Aires. The series gathered as "Church in a Revolutionary World" was presented in full in Montevideo and in part in Buenos Aires. And, the "Peace"
series was only presented in part in Montevideo and not in Buenos Aires.

Aside from the formal lectures, Yoder also spoke in many other loca-
tions and contexts. For example, he attended a week-long conference—the
first of its kind—sponsored by the Fellowship of Reconciliation in Latin
America on the theme "Christian Nonviolence and the Latin American

4. For a fuller account of Yoder's development prior to these lectures, see Mark
Thiessen Nation, *John Howard Yoder: Mennonite Patience, Evangelical Witness, Catholic
Convictions* (Grand Rapids: Eerdmans, 2006), 1–29, and Earl Zimmerman, *Practicing the
Politics of Jesus: The Origins and Significance of John Howard Yoder's Social Ethics* (Telford,
PA: Cascadia, 2007).

5. As indicated by the occasional marginal notes, these lectures were originally composed in English and then translated by someone more fluent in Spanish than Yoder.

6. Yoder had also been teaching part-time at the Mennonite Biblical Seminary
(Elkhart, IN) for six years and, immediately preceding his trip, he had taught full-time
for one year at Goshen Biblical Seminary (Goshen, IN) while continuing his role as a
consultant at the Board of Missions.

Revolution." He also met with Mennonite church leaders in both Uruguay and Argentina, with youth and student groups in Buenos Aires and Asunción (Paraguay) and with various people in the German-speaking Mennonite colonies in Asunción (including a visit to the Friesland colony and the Paraguay leprosarium) and in South Brazil. Further, he preached, on average, twice per Sunday in Spanish-speaking Mennonite churches, in German-speaking Mennonite churches, and Methodist churches.[7]

Reflecting on his experience several months later, Yoder wrote a follow-up letter to José Míguez-Bonino that described what animated his interest in accepting the invitation: "My entire trip confirmed the expectations with which I undertook it, namely, that in my not being acquainted with Latin America I was out of touch with the most exciting part of the life of the Christian Church, and that your part of the world is one in which the rediscovery of the vision of the Free Church is most relevant."[8] As this brief note indicates, there is no question that this trip to Latin America left a lasting impact on Yoder. Not only did it provide him with an opportunity to speak with Mennonites in significantly different cultural contexts, it also forced him to begin to learn about the particular forms of oppression—and the Christian responses to oppression—in Latin America.

Therefore, these lectures provide an initial glimpse into Yoder's understanding of the Latin American situation. But they are not the last word. Repeatedly, for many years, Yoder would revisit the challenges concerning the witness of the church amidst an increasingly revolutionary context, challenges that are frequently recast using the language of liberation in subsequent years.[9] At the invitation of Míguez-Bonino, Yoder would also return to Buenos Aires to teach for the 1970–71 academic year. In this later context, several important and lasting connections were made. For example, the active engagements with Míguez-Bonino and Rabbi Marshall

7. In this connection, one ought to note that *The Original Revolution* is dedicated to Bishop Carlos Gatinoni, "at whose invitation the title essay in this collection was first delivered as a sermon in the Iglesia Metodista Central of Buenos Aires." Yoder, *Original Revolution*, iii.

8. Yoder, "To Dr. José Míguez-Bonino, Buenos Aires, Argentina, October 10, 1966," The Archives of the Mennonite Church, Hist. MSS 1–48, Box 32, file 13.

9. The personal appropriation of this category is perhaps most evident in Yoder, "The Anabaptist Shape of Liberation," in *Why I Am A Mennonite: Essays in Mennonite Identity*, ed. Harry Loewen (Scottdale, PA: Herald, 1988), 338–48.

Meyer enabled Yoder to place the questions of social place alongside the issue of Jewish-Christian relations. In a paper presented in this context—"Minority Christianity and Messianic Judaism"—Yoder argued that "the predominant Christian understanding of the relation between Jesus and Judaism is fundamentally distorted by the position of cultural establishment from which Christians observe,"[10] an argument that would eventually evolve into *The Jewish-Christian Schism Revisited*.[11] Or, as a further example of the manifold connections emerging at the time, Yoder was discovered by several Latin American evangelical theologians—especially Samuel Escobar and René Padilla—who would openly acknowledge a substantial debt to Yoder.[12] This influence, demonstrated through continued theological and personal connections to the people and context of Latin America, would eventually result not only in a critical rethinking of Yoder's theology but also in an affirmation: Yoder would end up becoming an honorary member of the Latin American Theology Fraternity.

The Shape of the Lectures

To return to this volume for a moment, it is clear that there are three discrete sets of lectures presented here. That said, their arrangement is intentional in that each subsequent series builds upon the previous.

The initial and shortest series—"The Believers Church"—seeks to demonstrate that it is precisely the believers church, the free church, that can best remain faithful to Jesus Christ amidst the many challenges facing Latin American churches. Addressing the particular practices of baptism, binding and loosing, the Eucharist, and discipleship,[13] Yoder systematically argues that only the free church can (a) offer true religious liberty and maintain its missionary character over the generations, (b) restore the real

10. Yoder, "Minority Christianity and Messianic Judaism," The Archives of the Mennonite Church, Hist. MSS 1-48, Box 201, file "Buenos Aires."

11. Yoder, *The Jewish-Christian Schism Revisited*, eds. Michael G. Cartwright and Peter Ochs (Grand Rapids: Eerdmans, 2003).

12. See Samuel Escobar, "Latin America and Anabaptist Theology," in *Engaging Anabaptism: Conversations with a Radical Tradition*, ed. John D. Roth (Scottdale, PA: Herald, 2010) 75–88.

13. One might almost want to consider these chapters as the very early seeds from which *Body Politics* would later mature. See Yoder, *Body Politics: Five Practices of the Christian Community Before the Watching World* (Scottdale, PA: Herald, 1992).

person-to-person character of forgiveness among believers and, because of this, (c) call all people to live together in a community of mutual respect and to reorder their society in a truly human way. Therefore, he concludes that the path of the New Testament vision of obedience is found in community, expressed in community, and illuminated by a common hope. In short, the path of obedience *is* a witnessing free church community.

The contribution of the second series—"Peace"—is briefly foreshadowed in the first. Yet, because of its particular importance in the free church vision of obedience and the volatile revolutionary context of Latin America, a separate series of lectures is provided to flesh out both why peace is so important to the New Testament vision of communal obedience and how alternate visions of obedience undermine the New Testament vision and, in the process, the community of believers.[14] The first two chapters of the series present a biblical defense of love beyond the limits of reason and justice, a defense of following Jesus not based in a formal moralism or a literalist imitation but rooted in a vision of the testimony of what God is like that organically incites our fellowship with God and participation in God's work. These chapters are followed by another pair that outline what Yoder takes to be the two most serious digressions from the New Testament position: (a) the modern mentality of Reinhold Niebuhr[15] and (b) the ancient tradition of the just war.[16] To bring the series to a close, Yoder strikes at the heart of the issue he has been circling throughout: the question is not whether a Christian should be involved in the social struggle because Christ *is* and *always has been* involved. The choice is whether this involvement is done on the wrong side "after the fashion of this world" (which has been done for a long time) or on the right side with "substantial illumination or judgment from Jesus

14. In this series, Yoder's knowledge of the Latin American context is evidently superficial as his default examples are drawn primarily from the hostilities in Vietnam and not the indigenous context. Further, his comments concerning the European invasions of North and South America in chapter 9 may sound rather offensive to contemporary ears. That said, Yoder acknowledges his lack of expertise on the particular historical matters and one probably ought to consider these as "samples of a mode of thought" that could be reconsidered or replaced upon further review.

15. For an earlier and less concise form of this argument, see Yoder, "Reinhold Niebuhr and Christian Pacifism," *The Mennonite Quarterly Review* 29 (April 1955) 101–17.

16. For a mature and more developed form of this argument, see Yoder, *When War is Unjust: Being Honest in Just War Thinking*, 2nd ed. (Maryknoll, NY: Orbis, 1996).

Christ" (which is exemplified by the believers church).[17] In a manner that evokes the later *Politics of Jesus*,[18] Yoder challenges a variety of popular understandings of revolution and concludes this series with the claim that the way of the cross is the "most constructive social strategy for our age."

The third and final series—"Church in a Revolutionary World"—essentially seeks to explicate the claim that "What is morally lacking in the political revolutions of our day is not that they are too radical but that they are too much like the movements they oppose."[19] To this end, the series begins with an account of the course of history as a debate about the relationship between the church and the world that is immediately followed by a revised account of this contested relationship through the New Testament language of principalities and powers that enables a constructive rethinking of the victory of Jesus Christ and the distinctiveness of the church. Continuing the descriptive/constructive chapter couplets of this series, Yoder then turns to outline the connection between obedience and the fulfillment of God's purposes, the connection that is exemplified most emphatically in the kenotic self-emptying of Christ who gives life through the cross, the connection that is "the gospel pattern of social significance."[20] Practically speaking, this means that the way of the cross in social change includes identification with the humblest segments of society and loving concern for the adversary that begins in the covenant community birthed at Pentecost, "the most fundamental social revolution of all time."[21]

In conclusion, both to the final series and to the volume as a whole, the final chapter turns toward the relationship between salvation history and world history. In a final bracing yet encouraging salvo, Yoder suggests that the fellowship of God's covenant people is the fountainhead of social revolution—e.g., the rejection of racial and cultural pride and provincialism, the demythologizing of religious ceremony, and the democratic philosophies of modern times—in ways that are often mediated through expanding circles over generations (and even through the work of rebels).

17. See p. 93.

18. See Yoder, *The Politics of Jesus: Vicit Agnus Noster*, 2nd ed. (Grand Rapids: Eerdmans, 1994).

19. See p. 150.

20. See p. 144.

21. See p. 158.

The appropriate Christian response to this reality, however, is not pride but humility and patience, humility to acknowledge that the community of love is a gift from God, and patience to avoid identifying God's deliverance with the rise and fall of regimes. The claim that "if anyone is in Christ, there is a new creation"[22] is a claim that Christ has overcome the world. It is the "concrete historical beginning of a new kind of human society as well."[23] In this new kind of human society, the people of God are called to make their contribution to the revolution of *our* age, whatever age we live in. With this conclusion, Yoder has emphatically tied the three series together; with this conclusion, the free church and the way of peace it displays is, by definition, always the community that is the soul and conscience of our revolutionary age.

A Note on the Text

The present form of this volume represents the lectures as they were gathered by Yoder himself (including the titles of the three sections). Certainly, individual parts of and ideas contained within these lectures have appeared in other contexts. For example, "The Otherness of the Church"—chapter 10—was published twice in 1960[24] and parts of "The Biblical View of History" and "Constantinianism Old and New"—chapters 9 and 12—are combined into a single chapter in *The Original Revolution*.[25] Like *Nonviolence—A Brief History: The Warsaw Lectures*,[26] this collection of essays, as a complete unit, is an illuminating snapshot of Yoder's thought—in the midst of the challenges and turmoil of the late sixties—that provides a fascinating synthetic interweaving of diverse themes into a rich, complex, and coherent argument. In these lectures, we get a real

22. 2 Cor 5:17.

23. See p. 167.

24. See Yoder, "The Otherness of the Church," *Drew Gateway* 30 (Spring 1960) 151–60; and "The Otherness of the Church," *Concern* 8 (May 1960) 19–29. The same piece also appears in *The Mennonite Quarterly Review* 35 (October 1961) 286–96; and in *The Royal Priesthood: Essays Ecclesiological and Ecumenical* (Scottdale, PA: Herald, 1998) 54–64.

25. See Yoder, "Christ, The Hope of the World," in *The Original Revolution*, 140–76; and in *The Royal Priesthood*, 194–218.

26. Yoder, *Nonviolence—A Brief History: The Warsaw Lectures*, eds. Paul Martens, Matthew Porter, and Myles Werntz (Waco, TX: Baylor University Press, 2010).

sense of the energetic, enthusiastic, and accessible Yoder that is working hard to come to grips with a familiar challenge in a new way, working hard to bring multiple theological and sociological themes together in a critical yet encouraging manner.

To preserve the particular vibrancy of these lectures, we have edited as little as possible. We have attempted to introduce gender-inclusive language and we have also standardized biblical quotations in accordance with the New Revised Standard Version.[27] Beyond these significant changes, however, we have edited the text only where grammatically necessary. And, although Yoder left several marginal notes in the original manuscript, all of the footnotes in this volume are provided by the editors and not by Yoder.[28]

In conclusion, we would like to thank Martha Yoder Maust for granting permission to publish these lectures and for her genuine interest in supporting our efforts to bring the fullness of Yoder's thought into print. Further, we would also like to thank Herald Press for granting permission to publish the lectures that significantly overlap some of the material originally published in *The Original Revolution*. We would like to note that this volume is not meant to replace *The Original Revolution*, but to provide a broader historical perspective for understanding it. Finally, we would like to thank Daniel Marrs for his energetic assistance in preparing the final version of this manuscript and Charlie Collier and Rodney Clapp at Wipf and Stock for both encouraging this venture and seeing it through to publication.

Paul Martens, Mark Thiessen Nation, Matthew Porter, and Myles Werntz
May 2011

---

27. In the original manuscript, Yoder would often loosely translate or paraphrase biblical passages and, at other times, he would simply leave a note indicating that certain passages should be inserted at a particular point. Where we have standardized according to the NRSV, we have provided the passages in italics (and this is the norm throughout the volume). Where we have retained Yoder's paraphrase, we have not introduced italics (and this has only been done where he is attempting to highlight an aspect of the passage not readily evident in the NRSV translation).

28. We have also taken the liberty of moving references for direct biblical citations to the footnotes, whether they were supplied by Yoder in the original text or not.

I. The Believers Church

1. Only Believers

IN THE MISSIONARY SITUATION of Protestantism in Latin America, it has been most natural to conceive of evangelical Christianity as a unity. Under the pressure of an ancient and anti-religious secularism, what all non-Roman Catholic Christians held in common was invariably more significant than what divided them.

But from the beginning it was not so. Students of the sixteenth-century Reformation have in recent years made it abundantly clear that there were actually two quite different Reformation movements, expressing two divergent conceptions of the nature and mission of the church. On one side, there was the Reformation supported by governments in northern Europe and Britain. Whether in the Lutheran, Reformed, or Anglican forms, these official magisterial reformations had in common a fundamental conception of the limits and the pattern of reform. They maintained, from the Middle Ages, the alliance of church and state as this was expressed in the church's support for the political goals of the local government and in the government's responsibility for seeing through the Reformation. They also maintained the identity of church and society as expressed in the universal obligation of infant baptism.

On the other side of the great division, even though springing from the same historical soil of the early Swiss Reformation, there was the position of the free churches: the Swiss Brethren, the Bruderhof movement in Moravia, and Mennonites in the Low Countries. These were the weak but courageous representatives of this other vision of the church's liberty, which has not ceased to grow in numbers and in spiritual vitality over the centuries.

I. The Believers Church

The time is rapidly drawing near when Protestant Christians in Latin America will need to face with growing seriousness this division within the Protestant heritage. During the first generation of missionary aggressiveness, and continuing as long as evangelicals lived under the pressure of persecution, every member of an evangelical congregation obviously had come to that position by deep personal conviction. But now, with the decrease of clericalism, the change in the attitude of the Roman church, and a growth in numbers of Protestants, it may soon come about that second- and third-generation Protestants will raise for all evangelicalism many of the traditional questions implanted in the ancient debate about the baptism of infants. Likewise, the growing numbers and social prestige of Protestants will place before them questions of social responsibility and the possibility of a kind of establishment attitude toward society which was not previously possible in these nations.

Still another aspect of the need for a clarification of the issue of the free church is the great strength in Latin America of the "nonhistorical denominations." These movements have neither a strong sense of historical perspective nor an outspoken concern for the sociological faithfulness of the church, although they are exclusively free church in their character and theological structure. As the strength of North American leadership is replaced by the intellectual and sociological maturation of indigenous leadership in these young movements, their attitudes toward culture and society can be expected to shift quite rapidly, as has already been demonstrated by the evolution of Pentecostalism in the United States. Therefore, it is not a sectarian revival of divisive character but, rather, an ecumenical responsibility for the spiritual freedom of the entire Protestant movement that leads us to suggest that the great theological challenge of the coming generation will center on the choices that need to be made at this point.

As we approach such a study it should not be assumed that our concern is to determine which denomination is and always has been right. With regard to a particular issue, such as the baptism of infants, it is true that theological responsibility demands that we not be satisfied with affirming two equally valid but contradictory answers. Yet, neither of the traditions currently represented in Latin America has come there straight from the New Testament. On one hand, the pedobaptist Protestant traditions (Waldensian, Lutheran, Presbyterian, and Methodist) brought with them a form developed in Europe in the age of Protestant establishment at its height. Its maintenance in a free church missionary situation, although perhaps logically a contradiction, has not fundamentally changed the stance of the churches in society thus far. On the other hand, the North American believers-baptist groups have come to faith in a society for which, by a similarly paradoxical contradiction, the baptism of adults has become the established form of Protestantism in spite of formal separation of church and state. Thus, neither group has created a form of church life directly out of the Latin American situation. They have taken account of neither the Catholic conservatism of the past nor the revolutionary secularism that is now breaking in upon us. Therefore, although we deal with matters which historically have been expressed in the form of debate between denominations, let us not undertake them under any such immediately polemical assumptions.

Historic contestation over infant baptism has usually been made unfruitful by two mistakes:

a. On the one hand, in the Reformation era and ever since, it has been possible (and has in fact seemed most normal) to carry on a discussion of whether infants should be baptized as an isolated issue within the theology of the sacraments, a discussion seeking to decide the question solely on the basis of texts in the New Testament dealing specifically with baptism as authorized by Christ and as it is practiced by the apostles. While this kind of study is not completely inappropriate, it has also been largely fruitless because it placed the conversation in too narrow a frame. Far more is at stake than the proper handling of a ritual; the entire nature of the church and her place in the world is the issue.

b. The second misunderstanding has been just as harmful. Reformation debates about this issue began at the same time that Europeans were coming to conceive of themselves more and more as individuals. The Reformers themselves mightily fostered this humanistic individualism in their interpretations of the nature of faith and of revelation, but they retained the outward character of the institutions of Christendom in the sociology of their Reformations. It was normal that on both sides of the debate the question of infant baptism was understood consciously as concentrated upon the inward and individual experience. This concentration on the character of the experience of the individual was furthered immensely by the continuing argument around the topic of baptism in the following centuries. What it means to believe truly, what personal understanding and experiences are involved, how one can be sure that one has been forgiven—all such discussion tended in the direction of individualism which seemed to fit in well with the modern Western view of the person as a sovereign, and perhaps lonely, individual.

Again, this kind of study is not inappropriate. It continues to be theologically necessary. But, it is not at the center of the definition of the free church.

The Children of Abraham

The father of the community of the covenant, according to the New Testament as well as the Old, is Abraham, who forsook the earthly city in order to undertake a pilgrimage to the city of God. In quite separate portions of the New Testament, it is striking how uniformly we find the meaning of Abraham shifted away from the Judaistic understanding in order to state the nature of the community of the new covenant.

The first of these statements is in the beginning of the gospel story where John the Baptist was preaching the baptism of repentance. His audience at that moment was formed by Pharisees and Sadducees coming for baptism. He questioned their readiness to receive this sign of repentance: "*Do not presume to say to yourselves, 'We have Abraham as our ancestor'; for I tell you, God is able from these stones to raise up children to Abraham.*"[1] In other words, to be a child of Abraham is no longer guaranteed automatically by one's simple hereditary connection to the people of Israel according to the flesh, nor even by a position of prominence in that people. To be a child of Abraham is a miracle, worked by God with no more human collaboration than is provided by a stone, a miracle reflecting itself in a new kind of life, namely in works "*worthy of repentance.*"[2] John is not preaching individualism; he is picturing a new kind of community whose common basis is a novel renewing work of God and not a common family heritage.

1   Matt 3:9. See also Luke 3:8.
2   Matt 3:8.

In a quite different context as reported in John's Gospel, Jesus himself discusses the same topic with the Jews:

> *"If you continue in my word, you are truly my disciples; and you will know the truth, and the truth will make you free." They answered him, "We are descendants of Abraham and have never been slaves to anyone." Jesus answered them, "Very truly, I tell you, everyone who commits sin is a slave to sin . . . So if the Son makes you free, you will be free indeed . . . If you were Abraham's children, you would be doing what Abraham did."*[3]

Again the contrast is the same. The true child of Abraham will, like Abraham, believe and obey God. He who does not believe and obey in this manner, whatever his genealogy, is not a son of Abraham but of the devil.[4] Thus, sonship is identical with liberty; to be a Jew who is not a child of Abraham by faith and obedience is to be a slave to sin.

The third recurrence of the same pattern of thought is found again in a quite different connection, as Paul instructs the Christians of Galatia concerning the meaning of justification by faith. The promise given to Abraham was a promise based upon his faith. God was bound not to the law, not to the mechanical succession of children from father, but to the spiritual succession of believing obedience. Those who rest in faith are the true sons of Abraham.[5] The promise of the covenant, promulgated in the day of Abraham, is ratified and made fully valid only in Christ whose response was perfect obedience and through him in those who believe.

> *For in Christ Jesus you are all children of God through faith. As many of you as were baptized into Christ have clothed yourselves with Christ. There is no longer Jew or Greek, there is no longer slave or free, there is no longer male and female; for all of you are one in Christ Jesus. And if you belong to Christ, then you are Abraham's offspring, heirs according to the promise.*[6]

Although the immediate issues with which Jesus and the writers were concerned in these three New Testament texts are varied, the presence of this striking parallelism of thought is evidence that it was not only a device of rhetoric or argument to which a preacher like Jesus or John or a

3   John 8:31–34, 39.
4   See John 8:44.
5   See Gal 3:7-9.
6   Gal 3:26–29.

teacher like Paul would refer just once in order to illustrate an argument. This was probably a standard line of thought in all of the New Testament church which, of course, needed to encounter the challenge of Judaism in every city.

What is here described is not individualism but a new kind of community, not a concentration upon the inner experience of guilt and forgiveness which an individual may feel but the incorporation of that individual into a fellowship of the forgiving and the forgiven. Certainly, in an age when modern individuals become more fully conscious of their personalities as individuals and of their feelings and consciousness as modern individuals, it will be appropriate that the increased consciousness of individual personality will find expression and meaning that coming to faith and baptism will have for the individual. But, to center our attention upon the fact that the baptism of individuals is especially fitting in the age of modern individualism and personalism is to shift the focus of the New Testament concern.

Also, at those points in the New Testament witness where baptism is not the issue, it is just as clear that we are to understand the meaning of the gospel as summed up in the creation of a new kind of community. When, in 1 Peter 2, the Christian fellowship is called a chosen race, a royal priesthood, a peculiar people, and told by an application of a quotation from the prophet Hosea that to "be now my people" is the equivalent of "having received grace," the message is the same.[7] The church of the New Testament does not simply pick up the heritage of Judaism according to the flesh and apply the same principle of ethnic continuity to a group founded upon a new doctrine. Rather, it creates a new principle of community and continuity.

Once again the same point is clear in Ephesians 3. Here, the apostle Paul describes the truth that both the abolition of the distinction between Jew and Greek and the rejection of the flesh and the law are ways of maintaining the identity of the people as a mystery. This mystery stands at the center of the divine purpose uniquely revealed to him in his ministry as apostle to the Gentiles.[8]

Thus, our understanding of what it means that the church in the New Testament is the church of committed believers must begin with the mi-

7　See 1 Pet 2:9–10 and Hosea 1:9.

8　See Eph 3:2–6.

raculous character of the community of faith in which people of all kinds belong without distinction, if they only believe. We shall not center our attention on the emotions or on the information upon which belief often centers (although naturally humans are the kind of beings who cannot believe without emotions or information). The fundamental definition of the free church is not found in the feelings individuals have had upon entering it but in its character as a community founded upon the redemptive activity of God in Jesus Christ through the Holy Spirit with its order based only upon that divine work.

The Missionary Community

Only the believers church can maintain its missionary character over the generations. For such a church continues in every generation to be dependent upon evangelization, unable to survive unless even the children of believers are won by gospel preaching to an adhesion that is not taken for granted. Otherwise, if the children of believers are thought of as already within the community of faith, the unavoidable result is that within two or three generations the focus of attention changes from winning those outside the people of God to educating and holding those who were born into Christian families. With the passage of time, this always resulted in the geographic identification of one area as Christian and of other areas as pagan, or of one racial group as Christian and others as pagan. Other deformations also tend to reinstate the spiritual equivalent of Judaism, namely, believing that the people of God is preserved by its external order and by the control that the older generation and the inherited law have over the youth. Not infrequently, this deformation goes to the point of Puritanism or of inquisition, not shrinking from the use of social or even physical coercion in order to make sure that everyone remains faithful.

It is certainly not to be taken for granted that the mere formality of baptizing only adults will avoid these deformations. But it is sure that if we insist that membership in the people of God is a matter of new birth and that mere conformity to the standards and behavior patterns and ideas of the people of God without personal conviction is no help, this is the needed safeguard. The refusal to baptize infants or the immature remains a most appropriate symbol of the refusal to forsake that missionary character that the church is called to retain.

The Fall of the Church

Ever since the age of the Reformation, Protestant historians have spoken of certain earlier events as constituting "the fall of the church." This was their way of explaining how it could have come to pass that Roman Catholicism in the Middle Ages was so far from the life of the New Testament church that the only way it could find renewal was apparently through conflict and division.

In this evaluation of the fallenness of the medieval church, all Protestants and numerous Catholics agreed. But, opinions were different as to what it was that constituted the fall. Certainly, it was not the simple fact that the church began to be tolerated in the age of Constantine. For some, the essential errors were specifically doctrinal or ritual: the development of the idea of the mass as a sacrifice or of salvation through works. For others, the issue was institutional.

Others have felt that what was basically wrong was the development of a church order centering in the papacy with the disciplinary authority in the bishops. For still others, it was the support given the church by the state and the development of the Christian doctrine of the just war, according to which alliance of church and state was felt to be not only possible but appropriate, making not only defensive war but even the crusade a Christian possibility.

All of these changes were of far-reaching importance; any one of them suffices to support the sixteenth-century claim that the Roman hierarchy had sacrificed its authority to speak for the true faith. But all of these were simply the superficial and very logical outworkings of a more fundamental change. The basic shift in orientation that we most identify as "the fall of the church" was that the Christian community was no longer a community of faith, constituted by the divine miracle of repentance, brought together out of the world and living in the midst of the world with a mission to the world, but that Christendom had been created by the identification of the Christian faith with the total human community in a given geographical area. That geographical area at the time was the Roman empire; later still smaller units could be spoken of as the church.

It is this identification of the church with total society, rendering possible the use of the term "Christendom" to designate a geographical area and a civilization, which constitutes the most characteristic description (and the infidelity) of the so-called Christian Middle Ages. The organizational relationships between the government and the hierarchy, the development of the papacy, and the development of the sacramental system are all the logical outworkings of this fatal alliance.

Thus, from the perspective of the church of believers, there is a certain sense in which we can with gratitude accept the secularization that characterizes the modern age. To the extent that this means Christian faith is being disentangled from a particular civilization, a particular part of the world, a particular social structure, and especially to the extent to which it is being disentangled from identification with the total membership of any one special group or nation, this development "clears the decks" for a restatement of what it means for the church to be in but not of the world.

By this we certainly do not mean that the mounting tide of non-religious or irreligious or anti-religious thought is itself wholesome or saving. We cannot say that the entire process of secularization is wholesome or that we can derive guidance from it for how God wants the world to develop. But at least the dismantling of the misunderstanding of Christendom is to be welcomed. We shall have made progress if we learn to understand the faith no longer as the cultural possession of a given population but, again, as the call to a voluntary community.

One of the obvious implications of the dissociation of church and society is the demand for religious liberty. It has been adequately demonstrated that the believers church movement of the Reformation marks the real origin of the concept of religious liberty. Religious liberty is not only a necessary limitation upon the power of the state; it also marks a voluntary renunciation by the church of any capacity to coerce. Many religious bodies have objected to the authority of the state in matters of religion when it was exercised *against* them. Yet, it is only from the perspective of the free church that we find Christian thinkers also insisting upon the renunciation of the use of such authority *in favor of* what they consider to be the truth. But this concern for religious liberty, as important as it has become in our age, is likewise not the rootage but simply the outworking of the disentanglement of the covenant of faith from the natural community.

What is true of religious liberty must be said for the concept of religious establishment as well. The church is not the church of the nation or of the state or of the social order. It is present in the midst of the population and the social order and concerned for their welfare. But, often enough, its contribution is a proclamation of judgment. Its capacity to be the true church is often dependent upon her independence from the powers currently exercising sovereignty. So, in a socially homogeneous community, if there should be no protest against extending to a church the privilege of official recognition, even then it would be wrong.

Conclusion

The testing of the freedom of the church often, if not always, comes at some external point where the circumference of the life of the church comes in contact with the claims of the world. Thus, we may need to speak of the governmental recognition of church, of the issue of religious liberty, of the freedom for the individual to make one's own choice and commitment. In the same way, we can speak of specific polemical issues as we defend one kind of church practice against another. We shall continue to need to argue the wrongness of the baptism of infants. Yet behind or above or beyond all of this, the fundamental concern in our understanding of what it means to be the free church is the freedom of the Holy Spirit of God to constitute—in every day, in every generation, and in every place—that people of the new covenant whose daily existence reflects the reality that God has come in the midst of humanity to be their God and to make them his people.

2. The Commission to Bind and Loose

ONLY TWO TIMES IN the reporting of the gospel story do we find the word *ekklesia* from the lips of Jesus: in chapters 16 and 18 of the Gospel reported according to Matthew.[1] Both times, this is in connection with the authorization given to the gathering of believers to "bind and loose." The phrase is not a current one in our modern conversation. Yet, for Jesus and the New Testament church, it seems to have been of such importance that part of the definition of the church is that it is where this binding and loosing take place.

To understand the full significance of this phrase in our modern languages we need to use more than one translation. It often happens that in one language concepts can be brought together under one word which requires a choice between two different terms in another language. Where you in Spanish say *hacer*, we in English must choose between "to make" and "to do." Conversely, when we in English are satisfied with one verb, "to be," the Spanish must choose between *estar* and *ser*. In a comparable way, in order to understand fully what Jesus instructed the church to do with the use of these terms—binding and loosing—we must make two distinct applications in our modern context.

The Church Is a Community of Forgiveness

In the parallel passage in John 20, Jesus speaks in almost the same language, imparting the gift of the Holy Spirit to his gathered disciples, and

---

1. See Matt 16:18 and 18:15.

authorizing them to forgive sins; "*If you forgive the sins of any, they are forgiven them; if you retain the sins of any, they are retained.*"[2]

Thus it is clear that one meaning of binding and loosing has to do with the remission of sins. The church is authorized to speak on God's behalf, like an ambassador or an attorney empowered to sign a document in the name of someone else.

Our churches of the free church tradition have often taken great and careful concern for the holy living of their members. This was the case for the early Anabaptists, for the Puritans, and for John Wesley. In this history, however, it is not clear whether evangelical Christians always succeeded in making it plain that what they were doing when they expressed concern for the sin and the obedience of members was, in fact, reflecting the gospel by being instruments of forgiveness.

In the instructions of Jesus found in Matt 18:15, it is abundantly clear that the purpose is not to punish but to forgive: "*If another member of the church sins against you, go and point out the fault when the two of you are alone. If the member listens to you, you have regained that one.*" The normal outcome of this procedure of reconciliatory approach is that "*you have regained that one.*" The purpose is not to penalize, nor is it to teach a lesson to others that they might learn the seriousness of sin, nor is it to give an outlet to the resentment and the anger of the one sinned against. The need of the offender is to be restored, and this is the way to do it. Exactly the same procedure is referred to in Galatians 6:2—"*Bear one another's burdens, and in this way you will fulfill the law of Christ*"—and in Jam 5:19–20—"*My brothers and sisters, if anyone among you wanders from the truth and is brought back by another, you should know that whoever brings back a sinner from wandering will save the sinner's soul from death and will cover a multitude of sins.*"

The point of this instruction on the part of our Lord was not simply that his disciples would need ways of resolving social problems. It is rather that, if the church is to preach a gospel of forgiveness at all, this must be made real in specific times and places in the relations between particular persons. Forgiveness must be made flesh among people where it is needed.

We need this biblical teaching especially when we seek to build the church in those parts of the world that have been strongly under the impress of Roman Catholic practices. We need this teaching as a safeguard

2. John 20:23.

against purely anti-Catholic reflexes that lead secular humanity and some Protestants in the direction of spiritual solitude. What is wrong with the traditional Roman Catholic practice of penance and absolution, as it is routinely understood and practiced in popular forms, is not that a person forgives another person's sins in the name of God—this is a fundamental assignment given to the church by the New Testament and, normally, should be exercised first of all by one individual according to Jesus' own words.

The errors in the current Catholic practice concern not *whether* but *how* this word of forgiveness is spoken. Jesus indicates that it is the responsibility of every person: "If another member of the church sins against you, go . . ." This is a universal responsibility carried by every Christian for every other believer with whom one is acquainted. It is neither a ministerial specialization nor a sacramental privilege.

Secondly, what is questionable in the Roman Catholic practice is the prescribed relationship of the absolution to a process of penitential performances in such a way that the offender may think that it is the penitential performance which earns forgiveness. Further, everything that makes the Catholic penitential practice legally consistent, objective, and impersonal takes it away from the context of a living community. This is in contrast to the New Testament church where forgiveness was affirmed between believers as a social relationship and not simply as a divine transaction.

In the post-Catholic parts of the world, we need especially to safeguard the biblical understanding of forgiveness against its interpretation as a purely spiritual and solitary occurrence in the mind of God and in the mind of the sinner, mediated only through the words of preaching. When a person really knows that he or she needs to be forgiven, that forgiveness needs to be spoken by a fellow believer.

Although Martin Luther had no intention of radically doing away with the practice of aural confession, the effect of the Reformation was to make the practice unpopular. Martin Bucer in the sixteenth century and pietism in the seventeenth attempted to restore something of this element of personal humility, confession, and assurance. In a similar way, Methodism came into being when John Wesley created a way for the individual to experience, in the conversation of a small group, what it means to be admonished and forgiven. Today, in the Western Protestant part of the world, there are some who suggest that a large part of the popularity of psychoanalysis (which moves far beyond serving as therapy for sick spirits and becomes almost a substitute religion) is partly explained by the fact that the psychoanalyst hears confessions and imparts a kind of secular forgiveness by his very acceptance of a continuing relationship with the client.

But, it is not only the Catholic and Protestant mass churches which have failed to make this forgiveness real in the life of the congregation. The free churches, for their part, have been tempted to transform this process of reconciliation into a tool of punishment. Instead of speaking of forgiveness, we have come to speak of church discipline. It has been conceived of as a way to make the sinner suffer, to make the sinner conscious of having hurt the church, to give release to the resentment of the church, to demonstrate to others within the church the seriousness of the offense. Likewise, this procedure has come to center especially upon open and public kinds of offense rather than being an instrument for the discernment of the sins of the mind and the spirit as well. Thus, what was meant as a joyous reestablishment of the fellowship has too often become a rigid expression of the power of church leaders.

What still stands before us is a promise rather than an achievement of the free churches. Every revival movement has begun by reestablishing, through repentance, a possibility of communication among estranged brethren that had been broken off by the pride and the search for power of those within the church. This is our call as free churches. The free church is not simply an assembly of individuals with a common experience of personal forgiveness, brought about between individuals and God in the realm of the Spirit. It is not simply a practical instrument, a kind of working committee to get certain kinds of work carried out in order to evangelize the world. The church is also, in the world, that new people through whom God makes visible, in the most concrete form, that forgiveness is a social reality.

The Church Is a Community of Discernment

The other modern way of stating the meaning of the phrase "to bind and loose" arises clearly out of the usage of the rabbinic teachers of the time. To these scribes and teachers were brought problems of moral decision: "Is it permitted to . . . ?" The teacher who then spoke to permit or to forbid was binding if he stated a clear obligation, especially a negative one; he was loosing if he left the matter open or permitted the action which the pupil had proposed. Thus, the authorization given to the church deals not only with the offender but also with the authority of the standards by which an offense is to be recognized.

The two functions of moral discernment and forgiveness are closely interrelated. It is only because there is some clear understanding of what the standards are that sin can be recognized; it is only in continued wrestling with particular offenses and asking why they should be considered as offenses that the church keeps its understandings of what is right and wrong alive and practical.

The first clear lesson of Jesus' instruction is that the discernment of right and wrong cannot be separated from the situation in which we deal with our brothers and sisters and their need. We do not promulgate ethical generalities outside the context of their application. We do not identify as vices or as virtues whole categories of behavior without sharing the struggle and the tension of applying them to the situation of the believer who must determine how to behave when one really meets the choice. This is the easiest way to ensure that the church will not continue to proclaim standards that are no longer capable of application. The standards must constantly be tested by whether it is possible to convince a believer that he or she has sinned. In the process of conversation with the believer, if the church has been accusing one of sin when the accusation was unfair, the mutual reconciling procedure is the way to modify the rules. If, on the other hand, the standards by which the offender is judged continue to be correct, it is in the conversation with the tempted believer that the church will give the most fruitful attention to finding other ways of meeting those needs and temptations which led that person to fall. Thus, the redeeming conversation with the believer is the instrument of ethical discernment in the New Testament church.

The second clear statement about this process is recorded in Matthew's Gospel: "*Again, truly I tell you, if two of you agree on earth about anything you ask, it will be done for you by my Father in heaven. For where two or three are gathered in my name, I am there among them.*"[3] It is in this context of wrestling with fellow believers and their decisions that Jesus promises the presence and guidance of the Holy Spirit to the church. The

3. Matt 18:19–20.

Holy Spirit is described in the New Testament as empowering to obedience and as driving the church into mission. But just as often the Spirit's function is leading within the congregation in the discovery of the path of obedience.

It is this mutual pastoral responsibility of every member for every member, this "cure of souls" exercised by every believer as a priest for fellow believers, which prevents us from being led by anti-Catholic reflexes into a posture of spiritual solitude. As a matter of fact, in the sixteenth century, the first Anabaptists did not say that infants should not be baptized because they cannot have an experience of faith and the new birth, nor did they reject infant baptism only because there was no biblical text commanding it. Rather, their belief was that one who requests baptism submits oneself to the mutual obligation of giving and receiving counsel in the congregation—this is what a child cannot do. In the first clear statement rejecting infant baptism, in September 1524, before going on to discuss whether water has a saving effect or whether unbaptized children are lost, Conrad Grebel says, "even an adult is not to be baptized without Christ's rule of binding and loosing."[4] Thus, the issue is not the age of the one baptized but the commitment one makes upon entering into the covenant community with its claims on the believer. Likewise, Balthazar Hubmaier, the theological voice of the earliest Anabaptism and author of its first catechism, writes:

> Q. What is the baptismal pledge?
>
> A. It is a commitment which man makes to God publicly and orally before the church, in which he renounces Satan, all his thoughts and works. He pledges as well that he will henceforth set all his faith, hope and trust alone in God, and direct his life according to the divine Word, in the power of Jesus Christ our Lord, and in case he should not do that, he promises hereby to the church that he desires virtuously to receive from her members and from her fraternal admonition, as is said above.
>
> Q. What power do those who are in the church have over one another?
>
> A. The authority of fraternal admonition.
>
> Q. What is fraternal admonition?

---

4. See "Letter from C. G. to Thomas Muntzer," in Hans J. Hillerbrand, *The Protestant Reformation* (New York: Harper Collins, 2009) 170.

A. That one who sees his brother sinning goes to him in love and admonishes him fraternally and quietly that he should abandon sin. If he does so he has won his soul. If he does not, then he takes two or three witnesses with him and admonishes him before them once again. If he follows him, it is concluded, if not, he says it to the church. The same calls him forward and admonishes him for the third time. If he now abandons his sin, he has saved his soul.

Q. From where does the church have this authority?

A. From the command of Christ, who said to his disciples, all that you bind on earth shall be bound also in heaven and all that you loose on earth shall also be loosed in heaven.

Q. But what right has one brother to use this authority on another?

A. From the baptismal pledge in which a man subjects himself to the church and all her members according to the word of Christ.[5]

Far from being the extreme expression of individualism, the baptism of believers is the foundation of the most sweeping community responsibility for the life of all members. It is this process of binding and loosing in the local community which provides the practical and theological foundation for the centrality of the local congregation. It is not correct to say that the local congregation is of central importance because no other gathering of Christians can be called the church. The Bible uses the term "church" for all of the Christians in a large city or in a province. In recent centuries, the concept of local congregational autonomy has sometimes been misunderstood in such a way as to deny mutual responsibilities between congregations or between Christians of different congregations. We understand more clearly and correctly the priority of the congregation when we study what it is that it is to do. It is only in the local face-to-face meeting, with brothers and sisters who know one another well, that this process can take place, this process in which what is decided stands decided in heaven. Whether the outcome be the separating of fellowship or its restoration, the process is not one that can be carried on in a limited time and by means of judicial formalities. It demands conversation of a serious, patient, and loving character. Only when people live together in the same city, meet together often, and know each other well can this "bearing of

5. See Balthazar Hubmaier, *Balthazar Hubmaier: Theologian of Anabaptism*, ed. H. Wayne Pipkin and John Howard Yoder (Scottdale, PA: Herald, 1989) 350–51.

one another's burdens" be carried out in a fully loving way.[6] The church is defined by this process—not as a legal organization nor in a purely spiritual sense. The church is where two or three or more are gathered in the name of Jesus around this kind of need. The Synod, or the overseer from outside the congregation, may very well be of real assistance, but there is no way such persons could replace the process of binding and loosing community conversation.

If we understand the significance of the promise of the Holy Spirit deeply enough, related so specifically in Jesus' words to the church which gathers to bind and to loose (Matt 18:19-20), this may even protect us against certain misunderstandings of the use and the authority of scripture. One of the most enduring subjects of unfruitful controversy over the centuries has been whether the words of scripture, when looked at purely as words isolated from the context in which certain persons read them at a certain time and place, have both the clear meaning and the absolute authority of revelation. To speak of the Bible apart from persons reading it and apart from the specific questions which those persons reading it need to answer is to do violence to the very purpose for which we have been given the Holy Scripture. There is no such thing as an isolated word of the Bible carrying meaning in itself. It has meaning only when it is read by someone, and then only when that reader and the society in which one lives can understand the issue to which it speaks. Thus, the most complete framework in which to affirm the authority of scripture is the context of its being read and applied by a believing congregation using its guidance to respond to concrete issues in the witness and obedience of this congregation. Our attention centers not on what theoretical ideas a theologian separated from the church can dissect out of the body of scripture in order to relate the one to another in a system of thought. It is for teaching, for reproof, for correction, and for instruction in right behavior that the inspired scripture is useful. Let us, therefore, not be concerned as amateur philosophers to seek for truth in itself as if it were more true by its being more distant from real life. The Bible is the book of the congregation, the source of understanding and insight as the congregation seeks to be the interpreter of the divine purpose for humans in the congregation's own time and place with the assistance of the same Spirit under whose guidance the apostolic church produced these texts.

6. See Gal 6:2.

A Community of Grace

If we think of church discipline in the puritanical sense, as an expression of the narrowness of the vision of persons without love concerned only for an ideal pattern of life, then we shall stand before this divine promise—"*If you forgive the sins of any, they are forgiven them; if you retain the sins of any, they are retained*"[7]—dismayed at its hardness and afraid of its demands. But if we see in this promise of forgiveness the way of making real in the minds of guilty people the fact that God does genuinely forgive, then we may discover again (as has been the case in one revival movement after another through the ages) that it is precisely this opening up of believers one to another through which not only the immediate problems of personal guilt and offense but many of the other difficulties of the church can be solved as well. The only conditional petition in the Lord's Prayer asks that our debts be forgiven *as we forgive* the debts (the sins) of our debtors. Our Lord's only commentary on "Our Father" is to underline this same point: if you forgive others, your heavenly Father will forgive you also. The only topic of the rest of Matthew 18 is a series of parables about forgiveness. Thus, it is far more—immeasurably more than the mere formal restoration of one erring member or the maintenance of the church's discipline—which is at stake when we choose whether or not to believe that it is within the purpose and power of God working through the church to forgive and reconcile a fellow believer to myself. Might it even be the case that, in the effort to reach out evangelistically beyond the borders of our present membership, the churches have failed to retain within their midst that quality of loving fellowship which would certify that they truly do have a message for the world? In the ages before Constantine, the churches grew not because they were able to preach in public or to argue people into recognition of their guilt; it was the demonstration of the quality of life in the community that made others see their need and the power of God. Might it not be especially the case today, in a civilization deformed by legalistic and sacramental misunderstandings of the nature of forgiveness and absolution, that this restoration of the person-to-person character of forgiveness among believers could again come to be seen as our message to lonely individuals? An invisible God who forgives my past sins but leaves me alone in the present is not what

7. John 20:23.

I need; I need visible believers who forgive my daily sins, making it their responsibility to bear with me that burden. Let not the fear of mixing in others' business, or of legalism, or of Catholicism, hold us back from this most costly and most valuable gift of ourselves to the fellow believer. "*Go and point out the fault when the two of you are alone. If the member listens to you, you have regained that one.*"[8]

8. Matt 18:15.

3. The Mandate to Share

IN AN EARLIER LECTURE, we observed that it would be a misunderstanding to speak of baptism as a ritual needing to be administered properly. It is quite possible and desirable, in the right place, to deal with baptism in this way. At the same time, it is also an issue of profound importance for understanding the much larger question of the place of the church as a missionary minority in a hostile world.

In a similar way, we must carefully ask whether it is to be assumed that the sacramental observance of the Lord's Supper is simply a ritual practice to be observed according to the ordinance of the Lord because he commanded it and only because of the symbolic meaning which he gave it. In the early church, might it be that this practice was also the expression of the character of the Christian community with deeper significance than the symbolic? Again, we can only ask this question if we are willing to come to the New Testament divested not only of Catholic but also of anti-Catholic assumptions and reflexes.

Only one of the New Testament reports of the Last Supper—that recorded by Paul in 1 Corinthians 11—includes the instruction to repeat the meal: "*For as often as you eat this bread and drink the cup, you proclaim the Lord's death until he comes.*"[1] Centuries of debate have swirled around the meaning of the words "*Do this . . . in remembrance of me*"[2] and "*This is my body . . .*"[3] But the logically prior question would rather be what Jesus meant by "*For as often as you eat this bread and drink the cup . . .*"[4]

1. 1 Cor 11:26.
2. 1 Cor 11:25.
3. 1 Cor 11:24.
4. 1 Cor 11:26.

Since we read these words through the filter of centuries of church practice and debate, we obviously assume that he meant "whenever you observe the ordinance of the Lord's Supper." But, this is the one thing that he could not have meant. At the time he spoke, the Christian Lord's Supper did not exist and, therefore, was not a meaningful concept. Rather, the phrases "this bread" and "this cup" must have had one of two possible very specific meanings. It could have referred specifically to the Passover meal celebrated annually by the Jews, with the tacit assumption that the disciples of Jesus would continue to practice the prescribed ceremonies of Judaism faithfully. This would mean that there should be a Christian Passover service in memory of the suffering of Jesus once a year. The other possible meaning of "this bread" and "this cup" would be a reference to the ordinary daily practice of Jesus and his disciples, the common meal of the body of believers. Although this Last Supper was taken in a Passover context, it was, at the same time, but one more example of the common meal that must have been the usual practice of Jesus and his disciples ever since they left their other occupations to follow him and to share his life, his purse, and his table. The words of Jesus must have had one or the other of these meanings, or they may have combined them. The one thing that is clear is that they cannot be understood, first of all, as pointing ahead to the institution of an unprecedented ceremonial practice in the church.

As we move beyond the crucifixion into the early days of the life of the church, it becomes clear that the disciples' circle carried on the practice of the common meal. In fact, the risen Lord most often appeared to the disciples assembled to eat together—in the same upper room in Jerusalem, in the hotel at Emmaus, and on the beach at Galilee. The common meal had been the center of their life with him; it became the place where his presence with them was renewed. Therefore, the daily table fellowship of the believers' circle rather than the annual Passover celebration seems to have been continued as the center of the common life in those early days.

As this pattern of life was propagated by the missionary vitality of the young church in pagan society, Christians found themselves in dangerous juxtaposition with pagan practices that included religious banquets. Thus, it came about that new Christians in Corinth, bringing their habits of table fellowship into the church with them, threatened to change the nature of this communal experience by forgetting that it is a fellowship of the entire group and by concentrating inordinately on an exaggerated convivial joy. It was this distortion that the apostle Paul needed to right when he wrote to Corinth: when they met together it was not to celebrate the supper of the Lord but each was eating his own meal instead.[5]

What is important for our present search is that this Corinthian deformation could not have taken place if the ordinance of the Lord's Supper had been anything like what we make it today, whether in Protestant or Catholic circles, whether in evangelical or liturgical circles. If it had been a specifically ecclesiastical celebration, carried on according to the instituted forms for the specific reason that Christ had commanded that it be done with its meaning residing in what the bread and wine symbolically point to, then the disorders in Corinth would never have come to pass. (The abnormal is a comment on the norm.) Therefore, the presence of this distorted practice is the abundant demonstration that the normal observance was an ordinary meal taken together at every normal gathering of the young Christian fellowship.

Therefore, it is part of the definition of the Christian church that Christians are people who eat together. We profoundly misunderstand the development of what is referred to as Christian communism in the early days in Jerusalem when we try to see it as the outworking of a moral condemnation of private property or of a vision of an ideal social order. In the early days, the common purse at Jerusalem was not the outworking of the deliberation about whether it is good for disciples to have possessions of their own, and certainly it involved no speculation as to whether it is wholesome for society to be governed by a regime of private property. Sharing together was much more immediate and unpremeditated; they shared their wealth because they ate together and because food for the morrow is about all the wealth a common person can ever hope to possess in any simple society.

It is quite correct that, in order to avoid the Corinthian misunderstanding of the common meal as an overly joyful banquet, the apostle reminded them that the most dramatic Lord's Supper had been a Passover meal and that according to the instructions of Jesus it should be a time to remember not only his resurrection and promised return but also his death. Thus, it is appropriate that we should take the meaning of the annual Passover celebration in its Christian transformation into our

5. See 1 Cor 11:17–22.

understanding of the supper. Yet, for the early church, this did not necessitate any weakening of concentration upon the primary character of this celebration as a fellowship meal.

It is an irony of history that this reminder of the Passover sacrifice—when the apostle Paul sought to warn his readers against distortion of the simplicity of the supper by pagan admixtures drawn from the ceremony of the temple—could have had the effect, over the years, of permitting just what he wished to prevent. The idea of sacrifice contributed to the development of a quasi-magical understanding of the mass as an assuredly efficacious transaction whenever the proper words are spoken by a properly qualified officiant. Thus, what was initially a community experience by its very nature became a ceremony for its own sake in Catholicism, a ceremony that could be and often was carried out by the priest alone.

The Reformation was not sufficiently radical to restore the character of the fellowship meal despite some efforts in that direction, especially in the early thought of Zwingli. Preoccupied with the rejection of certain aspects of the Catholic practice, the Reformers were willing to agree with the assumption that the mass was a ritual distinct from the rest of life and debated only what it means and what it achieves, only what its substance is and of what it is a sign. They warded off the dangers of superstition but did not restore the reality of communion. The Protestant practice of the Lord's Supper remained a ceremony within the church with no direct connection to what bread and drink commonly mean. Upon unfolding the meaning of that common meal as explained in Protestant practice, it would occur to no one to sell a piece of land and contribute it to the church so that everyone would have enough.

The New Community

The point of this historical review cannot be to argue that it is possible or necessary to reconstitute the simple sharing of the band of wandering disciples or of that first Jerusalem congregation as a formal rule for all times and places. We do not need to argue that it is obligatory to modify in some prescribed way the practice of the Lord's Supper in gatherings for worship—although that would be an appropriate topic for study in its own right. But, between these two extreme applications, what we do need (and what evangelical churches in the modern world especially need) is a restored sense of the imperative that the church of Jesus Christ must be, as in the first congregational experience at Jerusalem, a community in which *"there was not a needy person among them."*[6]

When Jesus warned his disciples of the sacrifice they would need to expect, that warning was linked with a promise:

> *Jesus said, "Truly I tell you, there is no one who has left house or brothers or sisters or mother or father or children or fields, for my sake and for the sake of the good news, who will not receive a hundredfold now in this age—houses, brothers, sisters, mothers and children, and fields, with persecutions—and in the age to come eternal life.*[7]

Such a promise is a most striking occurrence in the midst of a text that (some scholars would tell us) should have eyes only for the end of the age. Jesus promises, to those who forsake all to follow him, a community in which the necessities of life are shared *already in this age*, in the midst of persecution. The apostolic writers could not have preserved this record in this form if it had not already been fulfilled in their experience; this was a promise regarding their present and not their future.

In recent decades, preachers and prophets have begun to see the *Magnificat* of the Virgin Mary as a charter for social revolution: *"He has filled the hungry with good things, and sent the rich away empty."*[8] But what some are tempted to forget is that this promise was fulfilled not in the mode of the expectation of John the Baptist—with a violent reversal of the social order from the outside through the tools of catastrophe, but rather after the pattern of Jesus—in the creation of a genuinely new social phenomenon, a brotherhood in which the rich give and the poor receive, not under the compulsion of the sword but under the beckoning of the cross. We need not ask why Christian civilization has failed to humanize the social order and has left the forces of social change to seek their vitality from pagan ideology. It is because the people of faith soon ceased to be—and even to promise to become—a community sharing the needs of the common life at a common table that radical social change in our day is the preserve of the pagan.

---

6. Acts 4:34.
7. Mark 10:29–30, emphasis added by author.
8. Luke 1:53.

One Lord, One Table

> All those who desire to break the one bread in remembrance of
> the broken body of Christ and all those who wish to drink of one
> drink in remembrance of the shed blood of Christ . . . must before-
> hand be united in the one body of Christ, that is the congregation
> of God, whose head is Christ, and that by baptism. For as Paul in-
> dicates, we cannot be partakers at the same time of the table of the
> Lord and the table of devils. Nor can we at the same time partake
> and drink of the cup of the Lord and the cup of devils. That is: all
> those who have fellowship with the dead works of darkness have
> no part in the light. Thus, all who follow the devil and the world
> have no part with those who have been called out of the world
> unto God. All those who lie in evil have no part in the good.
>
> So it shall and must be, that whoever does not share the call-
> ing of the one God to one faith, to one baptism, to one spirit, to
> one body together with all the children of God, may not be made
> one loaf together with them, as must be true if one wishes truly to
> break bread according to the command of Christ.[9]

One of the most general topics of ecumenical debate is the question
of intercommunion. A review of the several available attitudes on this
question may help to clarify the originality of the free church position.

The text just quoted, Article 3 of the "Brotherly Union of Schleitheim"
(1527), is probably the earliest confessional statement of a believers
church.[10] In the statement of the meaning of the Lord's Supper, its concern
is not with the significance of the sacramental emblems nor with the authority of the church organization or the officiant but rather with the right
by which each individual may properly be considered as a member of the
communion. It is appropriate that communion be thought of, primarily,
as the name for the group and not merely the sacrament.

Therefore, unity can only be celebrated when it exists. The unity of
the congregation and the proper belonging of each member within it are
prerequisites for and not results of the celebration. Thus, not only the
conditions of the individual membership are related to the communion
celebration but the disciplined life of the congregation has as its goal this

9. *The Schleitheim Confession*, trans. and ed. John Howard Yoder (Scottdale, PA:
Herald, 1973) 11.

10. This is commonly referred to as *The Schleitheim Confession*, although it is important to note the particular emphasis intended by the author here.

genuine unity that can permit the common breaking of bread to be genuine. The same "Brotherly Union" also says that the restoration of estranged brethren and the exclusion of the unrepentant also should take place "according to the ordering of the Spirit of God before the breaking of bread so that we may all in one spirit and in one love break and eat from one bread and drink from one cup."[11]

Much of the ecumenical scene is dominated by the Catholicized understanding of the Lord's Supper according to which the meaning and the validity of the celebration are dependent upon the sacramental authorization of the officiant and the technical correctness of the words that are used. Therefore, the problem of intercommunion is one of determining how different organizations using different forms of words or having different succession of authority can recognize one another. The numeric and emotional prestige of the churches with this kind of understanding, and their insistence upon institutional form, has led even some of the free churches to begin to speak of orders and of necessary episcopal succession.

The whole concept of sacramental validity, either for the priest or for the ceremony, depends upon a certain kind of philosophy. A particular conception of the nature of reality is necessary before one can believe that prescribed verbal formulae or manual gestures could—simply because this was thus prescribed—take on a specific metaphysical meaning. Such conceptions of the nature of reality are foreign to the mind of the individual in this scientific age. The individual will ask of a form of words: to what visible event do they point? The individual will ask of a gesture: how could it ever manipulate invisible spiritual reality?

But, it would be improper to challenge this concept of communion only because of the currency of certain philosophical ideas. The really significant reason for doubting the correctness of such a statement of the nature of communion is that it is very difficult to support it from a biblical perspective. The bearer of the meaning of the communion in the New Testament church was the body and not the bread. The failure to "discern the body," which the apostle Paul rendered accountable for spiritual sleepiness and death, was not an insufficient conception of transubstantiation but the failure to share the table with all of the brethren in the same church at Corinth. Considerations of episcopal succession and other criteria of sacramental validity, bound as they must be to particular times

11. *The Schleitheim Confession*, 10–11.

and places, are major sources of division among the churches. The cure is not to find an ingenious formula of compromise or a liturgy of reunification whereby the descendants of all can somehow enter into each other's organizational history. Rather, the need is to overcome the separation of the sacrament from the daily life of the body that was at the very root of the development of sacramentalism.

The alternative solution in the West tends to be the protestantization of the sacrament. In the heritage of the Zwinglian Reformation, modern Western Christians have sought to reduce the sacramental practice into what it means. For modern humanity, meaning can be reduced to clear ideas that are most correctly stated in words: the sacraments are parables or pictures which are useful to give dramatic completeness or artistic depth to the ideas they express, but the mature modern individual could best concentrate on the verbal meanings and would even, as in Quakerism, drop the forms completely. Words are, after all, more spiritual than bread and wine.

It is because of this conception of the sacrament as *communication* of the gospel that Protestantism has strongly moved in the direction of open communion. If the message of God's love is being proclaimed in these emblems, then it is the sinner, the person aware of one's unworthiness, who is most in need of this reassurance. The authority of the church to proclaim this message is universally given and needs only a minimum of external order which, in the origins of Protestantism, was provided by the government. Any church can be accepted which "rightly preaches and dispenses the Word and the sacraments." Mutual recognition between churches is no problem because both the church and its sacraments have been reduced to a message.

Again, we would not do well to argue, against this modern flattening of the concept of the church, that there is a religious or metaphysical dimension that it forgets. For instance, the traditional argument between the Zwinglians and the Lutherans about what kind of reality a symbol does have, after all, is not the point. What is missing in this conception of the Lord's Supper as a message, as an acted sermon, is the congregation.

Somewhere between these two competing conceptions is a third that many would feel combines the shortcomings of both. The Puritan conception, coming from an age when Protestant churches were a power in society, tended to make access to communion a reward for virtue. One asked the question of worthiness, thereby differing from the tolerant and modern Protestant pattern. But, this was tested morally or perhaps by agreement with a correct doctrinal statement. Like the New Testament church and unlike modern Protestantism, the Puritan communion is only for members; the members are measured by the characteristics of their own mind or morality and not by their participation in the life of the body.

We in the Anglo-Saxon world are experiencing yet another transformation of the thought of the Eucharist. In much of Protestantism, boredom with a word-centered service has given way to the thought that worship can find more meaning by turning not to the ideas but to their artistic clothing. More music, more careful choice of words, more repetition to accustom the mind to the world of religious concepts, deeper respect for the history of ritual and its solidity may restore the dimension of depth which modern scientific humanity has so nearly lost. Yet, the capacity to sense such a cultural lack and the capacity to try to fill it with artistic means already marks the class and culture, the needs and the capacities of a leisure class society for whom bread is no longer the normal food. In this society, one must give symbolic meanings to table fellowship because it does not occur to one to share at table with the congregation or with the poor.

Thus, we have every reason to return—from the preoccupation with succession or communion, with artistic depth or moral worthiness—to seek the restoration of that reality of which the breaking of bread in the early church was the integral expression and not an artificially chosen object lesson. Let a cell of that body be recreated in every place, composed of believers whose life together proclaims the Lord's death until he comes. Let this death be proclaimed, and let the universality of that communion be visible in every place in the reality of persons whose lives are wholly shared with one another and not by a definition in words or in ordination. Let us be freed from our capacity to separate the action and its meaning until our eating together truly means that our life is real communion.

Then forces of social renewal, like those unleashed in the first Christian centuries, may well go out from this table. Like the New Testament, the "Brotherly Union" (from which we quoted before) clarifies the unity of the church by speaking of its separation from the hostile world. Other theologies can define the sacraments without reference to the world, for the emblems and the ritual have their meaning in themselves. That meaning was defined in the age of Christendom. But, if the "one bread" we break truly points to "one body," that meaning demands an awareness of the church's mission in the world. The church is not an institution dispensing sacramental benefits to the population at large but a people called together for a mission in and to the world. Its separate identity is not a proud or fearful retreat but the presupposition of mission.

We already observed that it is the free church that alone stands toward the world in a genuinely missionary posture when renouncing a proprietary control even over children of believers in baptism. Only if one recognizes the line between belief and unbelief, between community and alienation, can the message of reconciliation be known. Here we touch on one of the genuinely live issues in contemporary ecumenical thought on the mission of the church in the modern world. Now that the alliance of church and state is ending, those theologies that were molded by the alliance would like to reestablish it by understanding mission only in the sense of a pedagogical service to society as a whole. Reconciliation then means a call to all people to live together in mutual respect and to reorder their society in a more human way.

If anyone questions the needfulness of this message to society, it would be a misunderstanding of what we need to debate. In the past, it has been the believers churches that have had this kind of impact on society and not those official churches to which one belonged by virtue of birth. But we doubt that such a pedagogical proclamation is either possible or desirable if it is not being made by a visible, committed community in which at least *something* of that reconciliation and social reordering— which the gospel commands and promises—is in process. Missions and nonconformity to the world are not alternatives but are mutually prerequisite. It is the city set on a hill that cannot be hid. It is where Christians will love one another—as Jesus himself asked it of his Father—that the world will believe.

In order to be understood by humanity, or in order to deal with their own common concerns, it may well be that Christians in our day will be led to change the times, or places, or forms of their meeting together. There is much to learn in the current ecumenical studies of the missionary structure of the congregation. But the deeper need, and one with which the disciples' church must help, is to rediscover the congregational structure of the mission. Let there be, first of all, a loving community of whom it can be said, "you have received Grace, you are God's people,"[12] and the world's capacity to understand will not be a problem.

12. See 1 Pet 2:10.

4. Walking in the Resurrection

> BAPTISM SHALL BE GIVEN to all those who have been taught repentance and the amendment of life and [who] believe truly that their sins are taken away through Christ, to all those who desire to walk in the resurrection of Jesus Christ and be buried with him in death, so that they might rise with him.[1]

One of the great unsolved problems of the Reformation era was the foundation of Christian morality in its relationship to the gospel: What does it mean to live a life pleasing to God? How can it be done? Why should it be done?

On this point, the medieval Roman Catholic tradition had been perfectly clear. The moral life is to be understood in terms of law and reward. There was no question of what to do. This was taught infallibly by the church and that infallibility reached right down into the life of the individual through the confessional. It was just as clear why to do it: fear of excommunication and social ostracism in this life or worse punishment in the next was the goad for the common man. For the religious, there might also be a positive call: the promise of social recognition in this life and the vision of God as an earned reward in the next.

Whatever must be said about the inadequacies of this social system, we must grant that it provided a solid basis for the teaching of moral obligation. It provided medieval society with something to lean on. It educated a whole continent, creating an entire civilization in which the notion of moral obligation rooted in the revealed will of God was fundamental. For the first time in history, it created a civilization in which God was conceived of as essentially a moral person.

1. *The Schleitheim Confession*, 10.

And what does the preaching of the Reformation do to all of this? If it is proclaimed that a person is justified before God because of faith and not of works, why then should works be needed? If, in the first place, it is impossible to justify ourselves before God by our morality and if, in the second place, God has chosen precisely to save sinners, would we not magnify the grace of God by accepting our sinfulness and ceasing to struggle against it so that we might be all the more dependent upon God?

Furthermore, the knowledge of the will of God is undermined. The pope or the parish priest no longer has a monopoly on the truth. Everyone can read one's Bible; everyone can know what it means to be a Christian in one's own vocation. Traditions are of no value; every one is one's own priest.

It is perfectly clear that the great reformers had no intention of relaxing the moral demands of God upon every person. And yet, by their own witness, the misunderstanding of the Reformation as a charter for self-indulgence was widespread. People became evangelical because they would no longer need to fast and pray, and sometimes because of the hope that they might no longer need to pay their tithes to the monasteries.

From that day to this, a deep dividedness has remained at the heart of the Protestant understanding of morality. On the one hand lies the clear logic of antinomianism. The law has been ended in Christ: we are saved by believing and only by believing. Let us love God and do as we please. On the other hand lies the constant corrective of Puritanism: restoring the appeal to the law of God and occasionally to the law of the state as well, restoring the idea that God will reward the moral individual and that Providence will punish every sin.

In these remarks, it is our task to ask what was done by the free churches about the problem of the moral life, its character, and its foundations. No statement that captures the novelty of this vision could be more striking than the phrase we have just read from the earliest Anabaptist confession: the Christian who shall be baptized is someone who desires to "walk in the resurrection."

A Morality for Christians

The first clear characteristic of this new understanding of the moral life is that it is not expected of all people. What had driven medieval

Catholicism—and was also to drive Puritanism—into a morality of law and recompense was the assumption that the church must be the moral teacher of *all* people. If a few individuals chose voluntarily to respond to the goodness of God with a life of love, that was cause for rejoicing. But, if they did not, somehow means must be found to make them be decent. The church, therefore, became more preoccupied with enforcing a minimum morality upon the reluctant than with describing the joyous obedience of the regenerate.

Christian obedience is not an ethic for everybody; the church has no illusions about being a moral teacher of everybody. Thus, the first originality of the disciples' church understanding of ethics is that "Christian morality is for Christians." This statement is by no means as self-evident in practice as it is in words. There is no temptation more widespread in Christian history than the concern to "make people behave" for reasons drawn from elsewhere than the gospel.

This is the point at which the spiritual movements of our age might create again a capacity for the church to understand a minority morality. We are not to ask how good it is possible to make everyone be or how to teach right behavior so that if everyone listens to us society will be helped. Rather, we are to describe that quality of life which this world does not yet understand but which is derived from faith.

A New Morality

The second characteristic of the morality of the gospel is concentrated in that one word, resurrection. Walking in the resurrection is a work of God alone. It is not a human achievement prior to the grace of God—as some common understandings of Catholicism could be understood to be saying, nor is it a humanly possible performance after receiving the grace of God—as some Protestant teaching would seem to say. The life of the believer is a miracle. It is one's dying with Christ and being raised to newness of life. Therefore, it need not be measured by what is humanly possible or by what we have a right to ask of a person. The measure of Christian obedience is the perfection of the love of God in Christ himself.

In the centuries when it seemed self-evident that a human could best be understood as a composite being made up of several elements—body, soul, and spirit, or mind, will, and emotion—it was natural that the transformation which makes the human able to reflect the divine will could best be thought of as a change in one or the other of these elements of one's nature. In the climate of freedom for theological expression in new terms that is fitting in the free churches, it was normal to attempt to strengthen this understanding of the miracle of the new life by theological definition. This is done when one seeks to describe regeneration and the imparting of a new nature in terms of substance put into or removed from human nature. The debate around John Wesley's doctrine of Christian perfection is of this character. In order to say more solidly that the new life is a genuine reality of experience and not just a mood or an attitude, definitions have attempted to describe what is removed or added to the composition of the person, what is eradicated or what new element is inserted by sanctification.

Today, we may no longer be able to speak with the same confidence in describing just how it is that a human can become a new creature. Today, it is unclear whether we can repeat John Wesley's *A Plain Account of Christian Perfection*.[2] But we must be no less clear than the Christians of another century were on the reality of that new life. We must concur with this concern to take the reality of the status of being a Christian with ultimate seriousness. Christians do not differ from non-Christians simply noetically, only by knowing about something that is true for all other people as well. The new birth is a change in being, not only in knowledge or in legal status. We must continue to find ways to say—as those Christians did in the language of their age—that some people are Christians and others are not, and that the difference between them is a work of God. Some people are members of the people of God and others are not, and the difference between them is reflected in the life they lead.

Holiness is not, as the Catholic and popular Western Protestant usage assume, primarily a matter of impeccable, pure behavior. It is a status, a relationship to God. But, neither is it, as some Reformation theologies and some modern existentialistic theologies would hold, *only* a matter of faith or of status before God. The holy life is a new kind of life. There are good explanations for the wave of criticism addressed to the pietistic element in recent Protestant life and thought, and to the overly emotional or overly individualistic understandings of conversion which some hold. And yet,

---

2. See Wesley, *A Plain Account of Christian Perfection* (Lake Mercy, FL: Strong Communications, 2006).

the corrective for that must not be to abandon the reality of conversion, which is not merely an event of human cognition but also a working of the divine spirit to change the character and the will of a person. Likewise, there are reasons for today's widespread dissatisfaction with a superficial moralism that identifies Christianity with certain patterns of behavior. Yet, once again, the correction must not be a complete relativizing of the difference which faith makes for action.

The Anabaptists, following Paul, chose to speak of this new life not primarily as discipline or illumination or purification or even as conversion or new birth, but as resurrection. Negatively, this explains why we are not helped by the words of the traditional Wesleyan language of the removal of the sinful nature. In describing this reality, parallels and pictures drawn from the old life are not helpful. The discussion of the resurrection body in 1 Corinthians 15 makes it clear only that we must say something about the novelty of a new order of being, but it is not clear what we can say. Therefore, we must disavow the excursions into psychology, or the refined distinctions of body, soul, spirit, or the notion of the eradication of the sinful will through which teachers in the free churches have sought to make real their descriptions of obedience.

A Morality of Participation

To say that the new life is rooted in the resurrection is not only to say that it is the work of God and that it is a reality which defies description in terms of human nature, but it is also to say that this new life is related to Jesus Christ in a unique way. In John's Gospel, Jesus speaks of this relationship interchangeably as our living in him and his living in us. The earliest fathers of the free church tradition, following both medieval mysticism and the humanism of Erasmus, spoke of this as *Nachfolge*, "following after," or discipleship. But whereas discipleship is characterized by the negative emptying of self in medieval mysticism and by a general statement of loyalty to the good in modern humanism, it means far more than this to follow Jesus for the free churches. With all the dangers of oversimplification that this involves, the free church morality is and must be guided by the idea that the life of Jesus is our pattern. Despite the dangers that beset the naïve, "What would Jesus do?" is still the right question.

Because the logic of such a position is accessible to the ordinary person, we often fail to realize how novel it is. All of Roman Catholic moral thought concerning right behavior is dictated by the light of reason and the law of God. If there had been no New Testament, the intelligence with which humans are able to understand the nature of things, added to the Ten Commandments, would still suffice to describe the good life.

Similarly, for most Protestants, the broad outlines of moral behavior are dictated by the orders of creation—the fact that the family, the school, work, and the state are instituted by God in creation and therefore binding upon us. If there had been no Jesus, our desire or capacity to be good might be defective. But what God wills, what he asks of the person who seeks to please him, would be just the same if there had been no Jesus.

It is only the free churches that have (not consistently but in principle) sought an understanding of Christian obedience as rooted in the character of God as manifested in the life of Jesus. If we are to affirm that God became flesh in him alone and was known to us as he could not be known through the words of God's prophets, then this must mean that *the life of Jesus is a revelation of true humanity*—as the Ten Commandments could not be—and a revelation of what it means to do God's will in this world. What Catholics have relegated to the monastery and what Protestants have relegated to the coming kingdom, the free church takes as a command.

To say that the life of Jesus is a revelation of true humanity is not a pious slogan after which we go on to figure out how to scrape through a situation the best we can. It does not simply mean "be unselfish like Jesus" or "be courageous in doing the right"; it helps define what the right is. Therefore, we cannot be content to speak, as many Western Protestant thinkers on morality are, about the structure or the context of ethical decision as if only the motivation and the modesty sufficed to make one's action Christian. We must ask about the substance of morality: what is right and what is wrong. We do not assume that everyone knows what is good and that Christians differ only in their reason for doing good, their energy, or in their modesty where they fail.

The widespread common conviction of Catholicism, Protestantism, and modern humanism (i.e., that the basic outlines of a good human life are self-evident to reason) can already be questioned on purely theological grounds. We could reject this idea in principle, following the guidance of a theology like that of Karl Barth. But that would not give us any new light on what to put in its place. If, however, our ethics are to be guided by Jesus, then we reject the morality of common sense or reason or the "orders of creation" because of its content and not because of its source alone. It is an inadequate moral guide because its standards are wrong and not because humans can understand it.

> *If you love those who love you, what credit is that to you? For even sinners love those who love them. If you do good to those who do good to you, what credit is that to you? For even sinners do the same. If you lend to those from whom you hope to receive, what credit is that to you? Even sinners lend to sinners, to receive as much again. But love your enemies, do good, and lend, expecting nothing in return. Your reward will be great, and you will be children of the Most High; for he is kind to the ungrateful and the wicked. Be merciful, just as your Father is merciful.*[3]

For a reasonable morality, the question we ask is, "What if everyone did it?" The question that Jesus asked is, "*What credit is that to you?*" If our life is a reflection of the working of God, it must be different from what is generally possible. Thus, it will also be different from what generally seems to be useful.

In the next series of lectures, we will be called upon to state the meaning of the command to love one's enemies at greater length. For the present, we should look at this command only as a symbol and a sample of the novelty of the life of obedience. We are not called upon to be guided by calculations about how best to guarantee an orderly society. Any such reasonable considerations would authorize us to distinguish between those neighbors for whom we are more responsible and those strangers who are not our concern in a reasonable way. But Jesus identifies the stranger, and even the enemy, as our neighbor. We are not called upon to prescribe the kind of behavior which everyone would find possible if we could talk to everyone, or which would lead to a healthy social order if everyone followed it.

The disciples of Jesus are called to obey him in a world in which most other people do not. Therefore, the logic of Christian morality must be a minority logic. Our obedience must be tested not by whether it can serve as a pattern for all people but by whether it is so different from the

---

3. Luke 6:32–36.

patterns of self-concern, which typify the present age, that it communicates something of the loving nature of God. We are called upon to love our enemies not because this is socially a healthy thing to do—although it usually is—but because it is the nature of our Father who is in heaven to love even the ungrateful and the evil.

It is not the purpose of the present lecture to discuss the pacifism or nonviolence that is the social expression of this particular aspect of the teaching and example of Jesus. But, for our purposes here, it is fitting to remember that the great reason for which most people reject this attitude is: "It won't work. People will not act this way. If they all did, it would be impossible to manage human society." So the question is taken for granted: "Will all people do it?" and if they do, "Can we manage society?" This is a question by which the morality of Jesus refuses to be judged.

Because God is most profoundly characterized as the Almighty who is *"kind to the ungrateful,"*[4] the accent in the ethics of Jesus is placed upon dealing with hostility and not upon the preservation of social institutions. For Jesus, the focus of moral concern is not the economic process of production, nor the priority of the family, nor the school, but what to do about the enemy.

This is not to say that one moral problem may properly eclipse all the others. Yet, it will be the case for every understanding of the Christian life that some problems are more central than others. For Jesus, the predominant concern is not how to keep oneself pure, nor how to be productive, nor how to remodel the social order, but how to overcome alienation between humans. It is not sexual infidelity, institutional inefficiency, nor laziness that best typifies what is wrong with our world; it is hatred.

Thus, it is simple logic when Jesus says of his disciples that his cross is to be the pattern of their life. He does not share his celibacy, his poverty, his pastoral language, nor his rabbinic profession; he shares his *cross* with his disciples and they with him. Thus, the same apostle who said, *"it is no longer I who live, but it is Christ who lives in me,"*[5] could say (when speaking at greater length), *"[We are] always carrying in the body the death of Jesus, so that the life of Jesus may also be made visible in our bodies."*[6] The morality of the New Testament is the morality of sharing in the sufferings

4. Luke 6:35.
5. Gal 2:20.
6. 2 Cor 4:10.

of Christ. We are not guided by a picture of the good society nor of the dignity of human humility but by the model of the brokenness of God as he came into the world to bear its sins in his body.

The understanding of this call to share in the life of Christ has not been served by those monastic and mystical understandings which sought to imitate Jesus slavishly or externally, e.g., in the barefoot itineration of the radical Franciscan tradition. Therefore, we speak not of imitation but of participation. We do not mimic Jesus; we live from his life: "*As he is, so are we in this world.*"[7]

In recent years, we have seen a massive renewal of the ancient debate about the structure of ethical decision in the Anglo-Saxon Protestant world. Are we guided by rules or by the situation? Is proper Christian behavior a matter of right reasoning from general principles—whether these be moral insights rooted in the nature of God or specific laws revealed by him—or is it rather a matter of loving one another and then doing whatever seems best?

This is a logically significant debate, although one finds it hard to understand the naïveté of those who seem to think it is a new one. But, it is not the debate in which Jesus and the writers of the New Testament are interested. For them, the concern was not with the form but with the substance of Christian obedience, not with how to put together one's thoughts about one's deeds but with the difference between right deeds and wrong deeds. The concern was not with whether to use principles but which principles, not with whether to act lovingly in the face of the needs of a given situation but with what action does truly express love and what does not. In the encounter with Pharisaism, Jesus clearly called for a certain kind of liberty. Yet, he explained this liberty by appealing to moral principles. In the unruly pagan world where the churches to which he wrote had to live, the apostle called for a more rigorous respect for a Christian understanding of work, sex, food, and honesty, but he did it in the name of Christian liberty. The debate between principles and the freedom to apply principles to the situation is a false debate. It is like asking which side of a coin or banknote is legal tender. This debate may be driven by a concern for a greater, more loving flexibility in meeting the needs of the moment. But it may also be avoiding the demands of simple obedience to the hard sayings of Jesus by claiming that they are not appropriate "in

7. 1 John 4:17.

the situation." To love one's enemy is often not "appropriate"; to bear one's cross is seldom "demanded by the situation." Yet, this is the Lord's path.

A Morality of Community

It would be repetitious to speak here of the ways in which the New Testament vision of obedience expresses and depends upon the believers church. It must suffice to allude to what was said in the preceding lectures on the subject.

The path of obedience *is found in the community*. Jesus' authorization "to bind and loose," as we saw, means that it is in the functioning of fraternal admonition and common search that the way of obedience is discovered. Solitary obedience is not the Christian ideal. Heroic loneliness in the right is necessary only when God's people are unfaithful. The norm is a common obedience to a commonly perceived duty.

The path of obedience *is expressed in community*. Jesus' command to his disciples to break bread together in his memory, as we saw, creates a new goal and a new means of social change. He has given his disciples the gift of a common life, and as they live together in love they proclaim what it may mean to live together in love to the surrounding society as well.

The path of obedience *is a witnessing community*:

> You are the light of the world. A city built on a hill cannot be hid. No one after lighting a lamp puts it under the bushel basket, but on a lampstand, and it gives light to all in the house. In the same way, let your light shine before others, so that they may see your good works and give glory to your Father in heaven.[8]

We need to be modest about the claim that our works are a light, yet this is Jesus' promise. He does not say that an *individual* can "witness by his deeds," for there are heroic pagans as well who can do good in a striking way. It is the community, the fellowship, which has this promise (and this judgment) laid upon its collective obedience: what the world sees of the gospel is up to you to decide, for you are what the world sees of me.

The path of obedience is illuminated by a *common hope*. The reason it makes sense to be different from the unbelieving world is not that we proudly hold to the law of God that will condemn others. It is not that we alone fear his judgment enough to avoid angering him. It is not only that

8. Matt 5:14–16.

we are grateful for the pardon which each has received individually. We can differ from the world around us because of the promise of the coming kingdom: *"Beloved, we are God's children now; what we will be has not yet been revealed. What we do know is this: when he is revealed, we will be like him, for we will see him as he is. And all who have this hope in him purify themselves, just as he is pure."*[9] Filial resemblance to our Father—sharing in his nature—is our duty because it is our destiny. Described as simply as possible, the Christian disciple is one who lives as if it were true that Jesus Christ is Lord. The disciple lives as if it were the Lamb that was slain who is worthy to receive blessing and honor and glory and power and not the tyrant, the banker, the proletariat, or one's own self. The disciple is one who has chosen to bet his or her life on the historically most uncertain conviction that, within the universal history of the human race, it is the Lamb who shall be Lord.

9. 1 John 3:2–3.

II. Peace

5. Discipleship in the Sermon on the Mount

IN THIS SERIES OF lectures, I have been asked to illuminate, from several different perspectives, that aspect of the life of the Christian which has been variously called meekness (by Jesus), defenselessness (by German-speaking Mennonites), nonresistance (by English-speaking Mennonites), nonviolence (by Gandhi and Martin Luther King), and "the way of the cross" (by North American Mennonite writer Guy F. Hershberger).

My intention in these lectures is to explain, not to debate. Yet, since this question is one that has been covered over for centuries by doctrines and practices in Roman Catholic and Protestant churches alike—the effect of which has been to reject the position of which we speak—part of our explanation will still need to take the form of argument. Even if there must be such an argument, let it be understood that our purpose is not polemic but expository.

Why is it that the early Christians, the early Waldensians, the free churches of the Reformation, the Quakers, and, in their train, the historic peace churches of today hold that the disciple of Jesus Christ will renounce violence and war in the pursuit or defense of even good causes? We must speak, primarily, not of *world peace* as a universal hope or a political goal but of the *way of peace* in our present warlike world.

We begin our study, as the New Testament does, with the earliest preaching and teaching of Jesus, especially in and around the fifth chapter of Matthew. We do not aim at a total or balanced view of the Sermon on the Mount or even of chapter 5. We draw from it only those elements that serve as an introduction to our assigned topic.

First of all, let us seek to approach these gospel texts with the simple openness of the new Christian of the first century for whom, as scholars conjecture, this sermon of Jesus probably served as a sort of catechism. We shall give attention later to the arguments of those who reject such a simple, believing approach to the teachings of Jesus.

An Ethic of Repentance

Everything in the beginning chapters of Matthew's Gospel is calculated to make clear that a new age of fulfillment is at hand. The genealogy, reaching back to the major landmarks of Israelite history, places the birth of Jesus right at the end of the third cycle of the genealogy. The narration continues in the same vein: the miraculous birth, surrounded by angelic announcements and recognized by the astrologers from the East; the ministry of John the Baptist, herald of another greater one about to appear; the baptism and the temptation with a view to the future ministry of this man; the calling of twelve disciples who in their number represent the claim to reconstitute Israel. All of this dramatized the proclamation that a new age is about to begin. But, for our purposes, it is sufficient simply to record that Jesus began his own personal ministry by announcing the beginning of this new age:

> *From that time Jesus began to proclaim, "Repent, for the kingdom of heaven has come near" . . . Jesus went throughout Galilee, teaching in their synagogues and proclaiming the good news of the kingdom and curing every disease and every sickness among the people. So his fame spread throughout all Syria, and they brought to him all the sick, those who were afflicted with various diseases and pains, demoniacs, epileptics, and paralytics, and he cured them. And great crowds followed him from Galilee, the Decapolis, Jerusalem, Judea, and from beyond the Jordan.*[1]

Repeating the message of John the Baptist word for word, Jesus says that the new age is dawning. Going beyond John, he demonstrates in signs and samples the healing power of the kingdom that has drawn near. The first and fundamental implication of this account is that we should expect Jesus to describe for his disciples a way of life which is new, unprecedented, surprising, and perhaps even unacceptable to respectable people.

---

1. Matt 4:17, 23–25.

Centuries of church history—both in the penitential principles of Catholic tradition and in the Protestant concern for personal integrity—have taught us to misunderstand radically what John the Baptist and Jesus meant when they began preaching, "Repent! For the kingdom is at hand!" Under repentance we think of remorse, regret, and sorrow for sin. But what they were calling for was a transformation of the understanding (*metanoia*), a redirected will ready to live in a new kind of world.

The teachings that follow refuse to measure according to the standards of common sense or realism or reason; they testify to the novelty of the kingdom that is at hand. Therefore, Jesus will be describing for us a morality of repentance or conversion: not a prescription of what everyone can and should do to be happy and not a meditation on how best to guide a society but a description of how one behaves whose life has been transformed by meeting Jesus.

An Ethic of Discipleship

"*When Jesus saw the crowds, he went up the mountain; and after he sat down, his disciples came to him.*"[2] When Moses met God on a mountain and received from him the tables of the law, this law was for all the children of Israel. When Jesus proclaims again the statutes of his rule from another hill, it is to his disciples. This is not a set of moral standards to be imposed on everyone or on the unconvinced. It is not proposed that persons using these standards can rule the unbelieving world accordingly nor that they will be prosperous and popular. The ethic of discipleship is not guided by the goals it seeks to reach but by the Lord it seeks to reflect. The ethic of discipleship is no more interested in success or in effectiveness than Jesus was. It is binding only upon those voluntarily enrolled in his band of followers. It is assumed that they will be a minority in society. How the world would look if everyone would behave as they did is not a question we need to answer immediately.

2. Matt 5:1.

II. Peace

An Ethic of Beatitude[3]

For many of the socially disadvantaged, the appeal that the thought of social upheaval has comes from a vision of the privilege that will be theirs under the new order. Often this vision is unrealistic. Especially in our day, many are experiencing that accession to national sovereignty is not as simple a blessing as they had hoped when they were being colonized. Nevertheless, one of the main motors of social change continues to be expectations of how acceptable the new order will be.

Jesus also begins his moral revolution by announcing who can rejoice in its coming: *"Blessed are the poor in spirit, for theirs is the kingdom of heaven."*[4]

With our heritage of moral bargaining—whether Catholic or Protestant—we have been led to misunderstand the Beatitudes as a scheme of performance and rewards. Thou shalt be meek and then thy reward will be to inherit the earth. Thou shalt be pure in heart and the reward will be the vision of God. This misunderstanding arises when we separate the beatitudes from the annunciation of the new regime. One cannot simply, by making up one's mind, set out to mourn or to be persecuted for righteousness' sake. Rather, Jesus is saying: "There are some who hunger and thirst after righteousness: GOOD FOR THEM! For the kingdom is at hand and they shall be filled. There are those who make peace; GOOD FOR THEM! For the kingdom is at hand, and it will be known that they are children of God." True Christendom is not a matter of earning a place in the kingdom, nor is it a simple blind obedience to directions. It is not doing what we feel like, nor computing how to achieve the best results. It is loving in such a way that, when the kingdom approaches, we find ourselves among those who are at home, who fit there, who are not out of place.

---

3. Author's note in margin: "Note to translator: Perhaps this term should be 'privilege' or some other term; you can perhaps correct the title according to the content of the paragraph."

4. Matt 5:3.

An Ethic of Testimony

> *You are the salt of the earth; but if salt has lost its taste, how can its saltiness by restored? It is no longer good for anything, but is thrown out and trampled under foot.*
>
> *You are the light of the world. A city built on a hill cannot be hid. No one after lighting a lamp puts it under the bushel basket, but on the lampstand, and it gives light to all in the house. In the same way, let your light shine before others, so that they may see your good works and give glory to your Father in heaven.*[5]

The Christian church is to be a source of light and of savor. Her good works are visible not for her own glory but to the praise of the Father. They cannot be concealed. Her deeds—are words. Later in the chapter, Jesus asks of persons whose goodness is careful and calculating, "*What credit is that to you?*"[6] In other words, it is assumed that there should be something about the behavior of his disciples that will communicate to the world around.

Thus far, we have been introducing the framework of the teaching of Jesus, that is, its presuppositions and its assumptions. But our goal is to grasp its substance, especially as it has to do with enemies, power, and war. This statement that the deeds of the church are a witness is a key thought. Our deeds must be measured not only by whether they fit certain rules, nor by the results they hope to achieve, but also by what they say.

What do I communicate to a person about the love of God by being willing to consider that person an enemy? What do I say about personal responsibility by agreeing to consider him my enemy when it is only the hazard of birth that causes us to live under different flags? What do I say about forgiveness if I punish one for the sins of one's rulers? How is it reconcilable with the gospel—good news—for the last word in my estimate of any person to be that, in a case of extreme conflict, it could be my duty to sacrifice that person's life for the sake of my nation, my security, or the political order which I prefer?

The idea that human life is intrinsically sacred is not a specifically Christian thought. But the gospel itself, the message that Christ died for his enemies, is *our* reason for being ultimately responsible for the neighbor's—and especially the enemy's—life. We can only say this to others if

5. Matt 5:13–14.
6. Luke 6:32.

we say to ourselves that we cannot dispose of them according to our own will.

An Ethic of Fulfillment

"You have heard it was said to those of ancient times . . . But I say to you . . . "—such is the structure of the rest of Matthew 5.[7] This has sometimes been interpreted as a rejection of the Old Testament in favor of a radically different set of demands. The Old Testament permitted hatred of the enemy; now Jesus demands that we love the enemy. The oath was commanded then; now it is forbidden. Just vengeance was required before; now it is rejected. And yet, this passage opens with a promise: *"Do not think that I have come to abolish the law or the prophets."*[8]

Let us not seek to solve the problem by the classical Protestant escape. Moving from another area of doctrine and another part of the New Testament, some Protestants have said that the greater righteousness—exceeding that of the Scribes and Pharisees, which Jesus demands here—is the gratuitous righteousness, the blamelessness before God which is imputed to the believing sinner *"not the result of works, so that no one may boast."*[9] This is the fulfillment of the law only in the sense that Christ is the end of the law. Its demands, impossible to meet and crushing us under their impossibility, lead us to the faith which alone saves.

But if Jesus' purpose was to teach the uselessness of works for salvation, he hardly needed to be so precise about the novelty of his demands. For the Old Testament law was already too much to bear from this perspective. It needed no sharpening up. So this application of the doctrine of justification by faith alone is no answer, for the question it answers is a different one.

This interpretation would understand Jesus to be criticizing the Scribes and the Pharisees because they kept the law. But, as a matter of fact, Jesus is reprimanding them because they make it too easy to keep.

But perhaps the apparent contradiction between fulfillment and "but I say to you" is not real. Is it actually the *LAW* which Jesus rejects as he

---

7. See Matt 5:21–48.

8. Matt 5:17.

9. Eph 2:9.

speaks of enmity, adultery, swearing, and vengeance? Does he take issue with either the text or the intent of the Torah?

In one case, Jesus directly contradicts the text that he quotes: "*You shall love your neighbor and hate your enemy*."[10] Now, "love your neighbor" is in the law but "hate your enemy" is not. In two other cases, he lets the older statement stand unchanged but enormously intensifies the application of its intention. The prohibition of murder and adultery remains. It is no contradiction for Jesus to discern the murderous or adulterous intention behind these forbidden acts.

An understanding of the other three contrasts depends on what the earlier law actually intended. The provision for divorce (Deut 24:1–4), as Jesus explains it more fully in Matt 19:3–12, was a concession to hardness of heart. But within that limitation, its effect was to defend the stability of a marriage and the dignity of women. Deuteronomy 24 does not approve of divorce; it does not even authorize it. It says that where divorce has taken place already, the rejected and already remarried wife shall not be cheaply thrown around as if her second marriage bond had constituted a breach of the first. This central concern of the earlier corrective is what Jesus now carries to its consistent conclusion, namely, that the second marriage, destroying the first, should not take place at all. Likewise, in the ancient Israelite setting, the formula "*eye for eye, tooth for tooth*" actually meant a limitation placed upon vengeance.[11] Vengeance could not be taken by the offended one or by the next of kin, but it became the concern of the authorities and was limited to the strict equivalent of the harm done. Thus, even though Jesus pushes the renunciation of vengeance a powerful step further, it is in the direction set by the ancient rules. In a similar way, the same concern for veracity and for limiting the quasi-superstitious use of the name of God—which had *begun* by calling for truthfulness in swearing—takes a step further *in the same direction* by rejecting the oath itself as a concession to dishonesty and as an abuse of the name of God.

What Jesus meant by fulfillment was thus a quite literal "filling full," a carrying on to full accomplishment of the intent of the earlier moral guides. Therefore, it is a most striking contrast not to the Old Testament but to interpretation of righteousness in the tradition of the Scribes and Pharisees. Since the Scribes and Pharisees were serious, pious, and well-

10. Matt 5:43.
11. Ex 21:24.

intentioned people like ourselves, trying as we do to get the moral teaching of their scriptures out where it could give guidance to the common person, it is not a merely historical exercise to ask just what their mistake was.[12]

The first characteristic of the righteousness of the Scribes and Pharisees is that it makes its standard fulfillable. Loving my neighbor is possible if I may still hate. Rigorously keeping an oath in the name of the Lord God himself is possible if I may still leave room to cheat a little when I swear by Jerusalem or heaven. I can perhaps refrain from killing and from adultery if I may still cherish lustful and hateful thoughts. Thus, we still seek to tailor our morals to fit our means so that we can keep the rules and thereby justify ourselves. The logical circle is vicious. We want to be able to justify ourselves by what we can do so we set our goals within reach. We construct for ourselves a manageable morality that we can handle without repentance even if it should not be true that the kingdom of heaven is at hand.

This temptation is still with us, especially with regard to the problems of violence and national egoism that are our special concern here. One reason most theologies want to replace the Sermon on the Mount with some other standards is just this: they want something possible, something you can teach to all your children and require of all your parishioners, a goal they can realistically reach. This is a very logical desire if our goal is to be the moral mentors and preachers of a self-justifying civilization, including a service as chaplain to its armies. Jesus' criticism is simply that this goal is not the same as being heralds of his kingdom.

The second trait of the righteousness of the Scribes and Pharisees is that it is external and accessible. We get it out on the surface where we can prescribe and proscribe specific acts as right and wrong. We cannot tell if the heart is pure, but we can identify murder and adultery. We cannot

---

12. Author's note in original: "A marginal note: Many Christians in our age, even those whose condemnation of Judaism was enshrined in ancient liturgy, are examining their tendency to misunderstand the Jews by seeing them only through the lens of a few polemic passages in the Gospels. In the broader historic analysis, Jesus arose and ministered within the Pharisaic wing of Judaism. The Sermon on the Mount is itself a document in the Rabbinical and Pharisaic tradition. What Jesus labels here as 'the righteousness of the Pharisees,' we analyze as a universal human temptation and as a Christian temptation. We are not making a historical statement about Pharisaism in the first century, nor a judgmental statement about some peculiarly Jewish vice."

make a man love one wife for life, but we can insist that the divorce proceedings be legal. Legitimacy replaces love as the standard.

A third characteristic is implied in the outwardness and fulfillability of the righteousness. The righteousness of the Scribes and Pharisees assumes a reasonable degree of legitimate self-interest. It can ask for self-discipline but not self-denial; it can ask for temperance or moderation but not asceticism; it can ask us to bear a yoke but not a cross. And so it is today: the limits of moral rigor lie at the point of survival, either national or personal. Do not lie—except to save your life or your country. Do not kill—except killers. In the Protestant West, it is traditional to accuse Roman Catholic confessional casuistry (and especially the Jesuits) of making too easy accommodations of the moral law to the needs and desires of humanity. But every tradition does this in one way or another.

An Ethic of Perfect Love

Three of the six examples Jesus gives, including the first and the last, are from the realm of enmity, violence, and vengeance. Thus, there is no violation of the central concern of Jesus if we concentrate our attention on this area from here on. The last verse of the chapter, and the portion which has contributed most to making the Sermon on the Mount a subject of systematic controversy, uses the word "perfect":

> But I say to you, Love your enemies and pray for those who persecute you, so that you may be children of your Father in heaven; for he makes his sun rise on the evil and on the good, and sends rain on the righteous and on the unrighteous. For if you love those who love you, what reward do you have? Do not even the tax collectors do the same? And if you greet only your brothers and sisters, what more are you doing than others? Do not even the Gentiles do the same? Be perfect, therefore, as your heavenly Father is perfect.[13]

If everyone had read these verses more carefully, there would have been less fruitless speculation about whether and in what sense Christians can and should try to be, or expect to be, perfect. This command does create great problems in theology and in the cure of souls if we take perfect to point to a goal of absolute flawlessness or of having come to the end of all possibility of growth. But Jesus is saying that we should not love only our

13. Matt 5:44–48.

friends because God did not love only his friends. As the parallel statements in Matt 5:45 and in Luke 6 make clear, we are asked to resemble God just at this one point: not in his omnipotence, his eternity, or his impeccability, but simply in the undiscriminating or unconditional character of his love. This is not a fruit of long growth and maturation; it is not inconceivable or impossible. We can do it tomorrow if we believe. We can stop loving only the loveable, lending only to the reliable, and giving only to the grateful as soon as we grasp and are grasped by the unconditionality of the benevolence of God.

This is one of the keys to the problems of war and legitimate defense. Every argument that would permit the taking of life is in one way or another based on calculations of rights and merits. I prefer the life of those nearest me to that of the foreigner or the life of the innocent to that of the troublemaker because—naturally, as everyone else does—my love is conditional, qualified, and natural. Jesus did not condemn this normal self-seeking quality—for Gentiles—but he says there is nothing new, nothing special, and nothing redemptive or healing about it: "*What credit is that to you?*"[14] Not only is perfect love not limited to those who merit it, it even goes beyond the unjust demands of those who coerce compliance with their will. "*But I say to you, Do not resist an evildoer. But if anyone strikes you on the right cheek, turn the other also.*"[15]

This is the origin of the label "nonresistance." The term is stronger and more precise than nonviolence, for one can hate or despise, conquer and crush another without the use of outward violence. But the term is confusing as well. It has been interpreted—by those who reject the idea—to mean a weak acceptance of the intentions of the evil one, that is, resignation to evil goals. The text does not call for this. The services to be rendered to the one who coerces us—carrying his burden a second mile and giving the cloak beyond the coat—are to the person and not to the purposes. The resistance that we renounce is a response in kind, a returning evil for evil. But the alternative is not complicity in the evil one's designs. The alternative is creative concern for the person who is bent on evil, coupled with the refusal of his goals.

What in the old covenant was a limit on vengeance—for one eye, only one eye—has now become a special measure of love demanded by

14. Luke 6:32.
15. Matt 5:39.

concern for the redemption of the offender. This is perfect love; this is what it means that not a jot or a tittle will pass from the law until all is filled full.

An Ethic of Reconciliation

Jesus fulfills the meaning of "Thou shalt not kill" by moving to the level of personal intention: "*But I say to you that if you are angry with a brother or sister, you will be liable to judgment; and if you insult your brother or sister, you will be liable to the council; and if you say 'You fool,' you will be liable to the hell of fire.*"[16]

These three phrases are not simply Hebrew parallels all saying the same thing. Significantly, the three punishments are of mounting severity, from the judgment of the local village elders, to the national Sanhedrin (the council), and to the hell of fire. At the same time the offense becomes more interior, from the spontaneous public expression of wrath to the more premeditated, more verbal, cold-blooded rejection of "You fool."

The most serious hatred is seen not in the act but in the inner attitude toward the brother or sister. Yet this is not the same thing that many moral thinkers mean when they speak of the primacy of the inner intention. In their thought, the idea is that if one's desire is that good may come of one's acts, or if one wishes to honor God, or if one is unselfish, then any action, including killing, can be right. But, the key intention is measured by the *brother or sister*. One cannot even worship God, the text goes on to say, without being reconciled to the brother or sister. Jesus does not contrast, on the one hand, the prohibition of killing and, on the other hand, the love of neighbor so that one could kill for the sake of the principle of neighbor love. Rather, Jesus fulfills the intent of the prohibition of killing by centering it—not in the ritual sanctity of blood, as in Genesis 9, nor in the absolute value of the person, as in humanist philosophy—in the fellowship between person and person, as mirror and as means of fellowship with God.

16. Matt 5:22.

II. Peace

Summary

We have only begun to read the Sermon on the Mount for the light it shines on the problem of war. We have not asked, as theological experts do, whether Jesus' command to turn the other cheek is a formal legal absolute or whether one can ever conceivably love his neighbor while taking his life. We have not asked whether these texts are the exact words of Jesus himself, spoken in exactly this form on one particular day on one particular mountain, or whether they were put down in the present form from the memories of the early church as a summary of his teachings. We have only observed the wider framework of Jesus' moral teaching: its dependence on the coming of the kingdom in his person and work; its expectation of novelty, of miracle, of visible witness; its derivation from the unqualified love of God; and its unity of motive and deeds. Seen in this light, the love of neighbor—even the unqualified love of the neighbor, including the enemy, to the point of readiness to suffer unjustly at his hands—appears not only understandable but possible, not only possible but the most appropriate testimony to the nature of God's love and his kingdom.

Ultimately, we do not love our neighbor because Jesus told us to. We love our neighbor because God is like that. It is not because Jesus told us to that we love even beyond the limits of reason and justice, even to the point of refusing to kill and of suffering, but because God is like that, too.

6. The Cross as a Social Fact

IN THE NEAT CATEGORIES of theological tradition, we have learned to place what we call "social" and what we call "spiritual" in quite separate compartments. Salvation takes place in the spiritual realm, having been achieved for humanity by the death of Christ as a perfect sacrifice, meeting the requirements set by a just and holy God. Jesus was a good and, in fact, blameless human being. But just what he did as a human—how he lived and what he taught—is not of crucial importance for this understanding of salvation.

On the other hand, what we call Christian morality may be based on the example and teaching of Jesus. But it can also properly draw from many other sources: from common sense, from the traditional wisdom of the race, from the observation of the needs and the stable structures of society, from sensitivity to people's need, and from the calculation of the kind of results we hope to bring about by our actions. Christian morality is very important, but very little (if anything) of the detailed understanding of what action is morally correct relates in any direct way to the cross of Christ.

For centuries, Christians have been reading the gospel with this division in mind. They have, with more or less success, been able to put everything in its place. This meant that when Jesus was understood by some of his hearers to be proclaiming a message that had to do with the social order in Palestine, this was a fundamental misunderstanding of his purposes. Therefore, we can reassure ourselves that it was part of their basic unbelief that led the Jews to misunderstand Jesus in this way. This identification of unbelief as mixing the two realms further reinforces the separation of the two compartments.

II. Peace

But such a separation never really succeeds, especially as recent scholarship has deepened our understanding of the concrete social meaning of the life and work of Jesus of Nazareth and as successive generations of students have read the New Testament text more and more independently of traditional dogma. It is not possible to read the gospel story for the first time without being impressed by the social and even political character of the threat that the presence of Jesus represented in occupied Palestine. But we have been so brainwashed by theological tradition that we cannot (most of us) read the gospel for the first time. Therefore, I must beg your indulgence while I proceed with a brief review of the evidence.

> *His mercy is for those who fear him from generation to generation.*
> *He has shown great strength with his arm; he has scattered the proud*
> *in the thoughts of their hearts. He has brought down the powerful*
> *from their thrones, and lifted up the lowly; he has filled the hungry*
> *with good things, and sent the rich away empty.*[1]

What we call the *Magnificat,* which we assume must express the submissive piety of a tender Galilean maiden, is, as a matter of fact, a revolutionary social manifesto. To be sure, it does not prescribe that the revolution must be a violent one. But certainly it speaks of a revolution and does not prescribe nonviolence either. The effect of that promised fulfillment for which Mary praises the Lord in the language of Old Testament prophecy is a picture of social upheaval, creating the kind of social order in which those who had previously been disadvantaged are now in their rightful place and "the rich are sent away empty."

At his baptism, Jesus was identified by the heavenly voice in the language of two Old Testament songs: the royal Psalm 2 and Isaiah 42, the first song of the Suffering Servant. These may be complementary or contradictory personages if we were to look at the entire Old Testament's text in each case. But, in any case, both of them contain kingly figures. Neither the king of Jerusalem (Psalm 2) nor the Suffering Servant (Isaiah 42) was to be concerned predominantly with the status of individuals before the heavenly judge.

This kingly nature of the commission given to Jesus in his baptism is confirmed by the temptations that followed immediately. The tempter says, in effect, "If you now are to be King, this is the way to do it."[2] The

1. Luke 1:50–53.
2. See Matt 4:1–11.

60

phrase, "If you are the Son of God" clearly refers not to a metaphysical discussion of the incarnation but to the authority of the king as son.

The offer of lordship over the whole world (the third temptation as recounted in Matthew) was not the only temptation to have a political meaning. When the devil proposed to Jesus that he might throw himself down from the pinnacle of the temple, the point was not that by a display of magical acrobatic powers Jesus would demonstrate to the people his exceptional capacities and, therefore, his religious authority. Rather, one must attempt to imagine what it would have looked like if Jesus had fallen from heaven into the temple court. "*The Lord whom you seek will suddenly come to his temple.*"[3] This would have been the most obvious way to proceed if Jesus had desired to present himself to the surprised populace as the awaited messiah.

Likewise, with respect to the first temptation, we have good reason to ask whether the proposal that Jesus might make bread concerned only the stilling of his own hunger. A person breaking a forty-day fast does not begin with bread, and certainly not with a whole field of boulder-sized loaves. We can at least propose, as a serious hypothesis, whether there might not have been a connection between solving the problem of bread (what we call the welfare state) and preparing his people for the coming kingdom.

If the only purpose of Jesus had been (a) to teach us true morality as the best of the rabbis, (b) to be only, in a face-to-face, personal, non-structured way, just one more person among humanity, or (c) to lay down his life as a sacrificial lamb because an innocent death was needed to meet the requirements for a work of atonement, then the whole temptation narrative would have been pointless. But the report gives us no impression that the tempter was wasting his time. For Jesus, it was a real option (i.e., a genuine *temptation*) to interpret his messianity in the form laid before him by the expectations of Judaism.

The character of his ministry is no less politically tinged when Jesus first establishes his claims in the synagogue at Nazareth (Luke 4:18). In a very persuasive way, Andre Trocmé has argued that Jesus was thinking quite realistically here when he proclaimed the coming of the acceptable year of the Lord, of the reestablishment of the year of Jubilee, the Old

---

3. Mal 3:1.

Testament's prescription for social renewal.[4] Whether this is clearly the case or not, we must at least say that what Jesus is talking about here is radical social change. The omission of the next phrase in the text from Isaiah, the year of the vengeance of the Lord, will certainly also have been understood by Jesus' hearers—who must have known the text by heart— as a radical shift of emphasis. Jesus sets aside destructive vengeance—just what Jewish hope and John the Baptist had been expecting to be most characteristic of the work of the Messiah—in favor of what he is to do for the lame, the blind, and the poor.

The calling together of a band of disciples to forsake their normal means of livelihood and to live with Jesus in a new kind of community is an equally clear social testimony. The fact that there were twelve of them with a wide scope of varying and conflicting backgrounds and person- alities—all the way from the publican Matthew to the Zealots, from the uncomplicated fishermen to the devious Judas—displays the claim to re- constitute a new kind of Israel. And the very fact that there was, from then on, to be a body of persons making the moral teachings of Jesus concrete was also the most fundamental social threat. This denies from the outset the idea that his moral teachings might represent a mere utopian idealism. As long as the social critic gathers no people around him, he is no real threat. If he assembles only nameless crowds around him, he is a threat, but a passing one, for crowds are fickle. But if he gathers a disciplined community of persons around him whose primary loyalty is to his way, this presents, for the first time, a genuine social option and a fundamental challenge to any society's satisfaction with its present order.

Our interpretation of the meaning of the temptation to make bread is confirmed by the central event in Jesus' Galilean ministry, which Maurice Goguel identifies as "the Galilean crisis."[5] This event was meant to be both the culmination and the end of the Galilean ministry of our Lord. His activity in teaching and healing had reached its summit in the miracle of the loaves. The populace, which had been following him in great num- bers, concluded that the moment of decision had come and wanted to make Jesus their king (i.e., to make him the leader of a violent rebellion against the Romans in a way approximating what the devil had predicted

4. See Trocmé, *The Nonviolent Revolution*, trans. Charles E. Moore (Farmingon, PA: Plough, 2007) 11–26.

5. See Goguel, *The Life of Jesus* (New York: Macmillan, 1933) 278–88.

before the political consequences of his deed). Now he could restore the kingdom of Israel.

But Jesus did not cede to the imperative of the hour, to the pressures of his situation. He did not exploit the available possibilities to be the agent of social renewal. He withdrew and, henceforth, concerned himself predominantly with the small circle of his disciples. For the first time—and precisely at this time—he revealed his glory on the Mount of Transfiguration. Precisely at this time, he revealed to his disciples that he was to suffer and die. Precisely at this point, *"he set his face to go to Jerusalem."*[6]

The week of final decision begins with a political demonstration on a grand scale: Jesus' triumphant entry. In the events that the church celebrates on Palm Sunday, the peculiar character of the political position of Jesus is still being tempted. He still stands before an essentially political choice. He is welcomed by the jubilant masses as the "Son of David" who was to come. He takes over in the court of the temple with a claim to authority which cannot be understood otherwise than as messianic, before which the crowds and the merchants fell back in unexplainable fear even though he stands in their midst alone and unarmed. We can hardly believe that the Jewish temple police and the Roman watch, both of whom are said to have had jurisdiction over the outer temple court, and both of whom were especially vigilant on these feast days, would have been afraid of a rope.

Now is the time: *"The Lord whom you seek will suddenly come to his temple . . . and he will purify the descendants of Levi."*[7] And yet, in the face of this unprecedented opportunity, Jesus decides as he had before. He had chosen to enter this place on an ass, a decidedly un-royal beast in that time. He weeps over this city that did not want him to gather her children. And now in the temple court, with the situation fully ripe for a *coup d'état*, he lets the occasion slip through his fingers and withdraws to Bethany.[8] No wonder that the Zealots and the crowd are disappointed and would soon be ready to trade Jesus' life for that of the rebel leader Barabbas.

6. Luke 9:51.

7. Mal 3:1–3.

8. Author's parenthetical note: "Following Matthew and Luke, we have recounted the entrance into Jerusalem and the purification of the temple in direct sequence. If a night separated them, as it would appear according to Mark, this does not essentially change the character which the two events also had when taken separately."

II. Peace

Although he rejects the vision of what it means to be king laid before him by the crowds, Jesus faces it as a real option, as a literal temptation. He does not simply say, as traditional Protestantism would have him say, that political messianity (as if there were any other kind) is irrelevant to his concerns either because he is only preaching pure morality, because he only came to die, or because his kingdom is only spiritual. The violent political shortcut proposed by the people and by the devil was a temptation because Jesus had come to his people with concern for the injustice of the structures of society and for the needs of humanity.

But the political temptation of Jesus is still not concluded. In the night of his temptation, what was going on when Jesus prayed, "*If it is possible, let this cup pass from me*"?[9] What would it have meant for "the cup" to have been avoided? What would have had to happen in order for Jesus to avoid the cross at this point?

Edifying meditations on Gethsemane have seldom raised this very obvious question. Yet, to deal with Jesus honestly as a real human in a real testing within a real society, it must be asked and answered. Without knowing in detail what other possibilities might have passed through his mind, we can hardly be wrong in surmising that what would have been necessary to avoid the cross at this point would have been a holy war of some kind. Immediately following, we read of the "thousand legions of angels" which Jesus could have called upon for help, according to the words recorded in Matthew's Gospel. We read of the sword that Peter had at his side and used for legitimate defense.

Certainly, none of us has a very clear idea of what it could have meant for twelve legions (a legion seems normally to have counted six thousand soldiers) of angels to burst into that garden. But, according to the testimony of Matthew, it was a live option for Jesus to respond to his captors in another way—in a way which would have had about it all the marks of the holy wars in ancient Israel—in which supernatural powers would have aligned themselves with the weapons of his disciples to touch off at least the holy violence through which God's people would be freed and his law restored to its place of rightful honor in the midst of a renewed Israel.

It is not a new hypothesis that Judas did not have the intention of turning Jesus over to the authorities, i.e., the hypothesis that his betrayal could force Jesus (in order to save himself) to precipitate that holy war

---

9. Matt 26:39.

through which Judas the Zealot expected the breakthrough of the kingdom of God to be achieved at the last moment.

So Jesus is from beginning to end *homo politicus*. Not only his preaching of the kingdom of God—could there be a more specifically politically tinged term than kingdom?—but also his deeds were of the greatest political relevance. It stood before him as an open possibility that he might achieve his social purposes through the means of political power, combining the support of the Zealots with his own miraculous capacities. Jesus rejected this possibility because that was what God did not desire *and this is why he was crucified.* The inscription on the cross identifies that Jesus was the "King of the Jews" as the legal reason for his execution. Political par excellence in his proclamation of the kingdom and yet apparently nonpolitical in his rejection of the seemingly obvious means of establishing this kingdom, Jesus died (as we still die today) because people refused to see (as we today refuse to see) that political can mean something more than violent.

A very obvious objection must be met before we go on. The effort is often made to avoid the ethical implications of the last days and deeds of Jesus on the ground that he *had to die* for our sins. It was necessary—Anselm of Canterbury had said it this way—that a fully innocent, incarnated divine being must die in order to bring salvation to humanity. According to Anselm, when Jesus rejected the kingly crown, he did it not because this was the morally right decision but only in order to die.

Over against this objection, one can already superficially ask why Jesus had to die *precisely in this way*. If all that was really necessary was that an incarnate divine being should die, there would have been many less complicated ways for him to be killed, perhaps in the massacre of the infants at Bethlehem or in a traffic accident. But the problem is deeper. To abstract Jesus' death out of the socio-political side of his human existence is to misunderstand the relationship of what traditional theology has called the two natures of Christ. When one ceases to regard the political decisions of Jesus as genuine human social-political decisions, as this argument does, this denial implies the heresy historically known as docetism (denial of the genuine humanity of Christ).

Another possibility is to recognize these decisions as genuinely human decisions and yet to deny to them any revelatory character: Jesus decided this in his time and place, but we shall need other kinds of guidance in other times and places. This position carries the traditional name of ebionitism (denial of the deity of Christ). According to the testimony of the New Testament, the death of Jesus was no purely metaphysical event as some doctrines of the atonement would understand it. But it was a perfect expression of ethical obedience (Heb 5:8–10, Phil 2). In the New Testament, the use of the term obedience is the simplest and clearest indication that this human behavior of Jesus is to be conceived of as revealing God's will for the obedient person.

But at the same time that it has become clear to us that a social and political character is inextricably part of the ministry of Jesus, we have also seen, step by step, that this kingdom of which he was the herald was different in kind from the tetrarchate of Herod or the rule of Caesar and Pilate. It was different from David and Solomon as well. It is different. The difference was located fully within and not outside the social realm—not by being spiritual instead of social, and not by having to do with being reconciled to God instead of with man—yet it was a fundamental difference. Jesus exemplified a radically different kind of relationship between people.

> *But Jesus called them to him and said, "You know that the rulers of the Gentiles lord it over them, and their great ones are tyrants over them. It will not be so among you; but whoever wishes to be great among you must be your servant, and whoever wishes to be first among you must be your slave; just as the Son of Man came not to be served but to serve, and to give his life a ransom for many.*[10]

Yet the fact that God chose to speak of his will for humanity in terms of a city and of a king, in ancient times and in the age of fulfillment, forbids us to follow one very widespread pattern of thought in our own ethical deliberations. Many will say that since politics in this fallen world is clearly a matter of violence, selfishness, pride, and deceit and, since Jesus clearly called his disciples to a life in which those vices have no place, the person who would follow Jesus must choose between one of two possibilities:

a. In order to be effective for good purposes, a Christian must consciously renounce faithfulness to the form of Jesus' work. Like others in the area, although we would hope less brutally and unashamedly, a Christian must also seek power, hurt people, accumulate wealth, and take life.

10. Matt 20:25–28.

b. In order to follow the path of Jesus, a Christian must renounce all concrete concern for social and political issues; one must withdraw, geographically or otherwise, from immediate involvement in the struggles of this world.

Later, we shall look at the inherent logic of such a position; here we can only say that it misunderstands totally the meaning of the ministry of Jesus who refused to make precisely that choice. Just as biblical faith and orthodox dogma forbid us to choose between characterizations of the work of Christ as human or as divine (because he was genuinely both), so also there is no choice between obedience and usefulness, between moral purity and concern for the neighbor. The kingdom that Jesus announced and exemplified was not a non-historical escape valve from the realities of daily experience. It was a new quality of life offered to people at hand, in the midst of life.

But Jesus was unique: what has his achievement to do with people like us? If no division is possible between the spiritual and the social, then, certainly, there must be one between him and us, between the ideal and the accomplishment, between Christ and the church?

Again the New Testament confounds our clichés. At the outset of his ministry, Jesus called together the twelve, a nucleus of a new kind of society. From the start his new message took on flesh in a new human community so representative of his will—thanks to the wonder of Pentecost—that a generation later it could be spoken of as his body. And the most striking parallel between Jesus and his disciple lies right at the point of which we speak, namely, that the disciple has a cross to bear.

It is not simply that the New Testament speaks of the life of the Christian as life "in Christ," the life in which something of his nature and will find expression in the obedience of his followers (Gal 2:20; Phil 2:5–11; 1 John 4:17). It is not simply that acceptance of the gospel can be represented as a kind of dying without explicit reference to particular moral positions (Rom 6:5–11; Col 2:20). Far more often the concepts of dying with him and living in him find a much more concrete expression in reference to the social suffering of the Christians.

> *Now large crowds were traveling with him; and he turned and said to them, "Whoever comes to me and does not hate father and mother, wife and children, brothers and sisters, yes, and even life itself,*

cannot be my disciple. Whoever does not carry the cross and follow me cannot be my disciple."[11]

Remember the word that I said to you, "Servants are not greater than their master." If they persecuted me, they will persecute you; if they kept my word, they will keep yours also.[12]

One of the most striking statements of this understanding of the Christian life was written by the apostle Paul concerning his own ministry: *"In my flesh I am completing what is lacking in Christ's afflictions for the sake of his body."*[13] But, all that he says here he can say of the total Christian community as well: *"For he has graciously granted you the privilege not only of believing in Christ, but of suffering for him as well . . . let the same mind be in you that was in Christ Jesus."*[14]

The cross of the church is a prolongation of the cross of Christ, as the church is his continuing life in his body.

1. *But if you endure when you do right and suffer for it, you have God's approval. For to this you have been called, because Christ also suffered for you, leaving you an example, so that you should follow in his steps.*[15]

2. *We know love by this, that he laid down his life for us—and we ought to lay down our lives for one another.*[16]

3. *As he is, so are we in this world.*[17]

The same testimony is built into the literary structure of Hebrews 11–12. The relationship between the suffering Christ (12:1–3), the suffering of the great cloud of witnesses (11), and that of the believers (12:3–11) is obviously the same unity that we have seen above in other texts.

Thus the heart of the primitive church spoke spontaneously. The thought springs forth even when such statements are not specifically necessary for the progress of the writer's thought. There is no specifically

11. Luke 14:25–27.

12. John 15:20.

13. Col 1:24. See also Phil 3:10 and 1 Cor 4:10.

14. Phil 1:29 and 2:5.

15. 1 Pet 2:20–21.

16. 1 John 3:16.

17. 1 John 4:17.

Pauline, Petrine, or Johannine thought but the common property of the primitive community. Christ lives in us: the life that we live in the flesh, not we live it but Christ in us.[18]

According to traditional pious usage, there is nothing new about the thought of Christians or the church bearing a cross. Much is made of this phrase, especially in pastoral care. If, however, we have ascertained that the cross of Christ was an eminently political event, then the cross of the church must also be understood in a previously unfamiliar light. In pastoral care and personal piety, the thought of the cross has been used in order to give individuals the courage to live with their rheumatism or their poverty, or to get along with a tyrannical mother-in-law. This is not the point, at least not the central point of the New Testament's constant reference to the cross that Christians have to bear. The cross of Jesus was no inexplicable evil that fell upon him accidentally like a contagious disease, a storm, or an earthquake. For Jesus—however much understanding and love we do want to express to the victims of sickness and accident—the problem of his life ministry was not that of the inevitability of suffering. On the contrary, his cross was avoidable suffering. It was the price of his obedience to the love of the Father in the midst of a world in rebellion. So must it also be for us.

The primitive Christian community had no power to decide whether it would take over responsibility for the guidance of the Roman state. It was and was to remain a persecuted minority. Therefore, it would be possible to explain the church's attitude as a solution born of despair, making the best of a bad deal. But it was not that. The church saw the path of suffering which it was to take not as misfortune which really should not have happened, nor as an accident which could just as well have happened to someone else. The cross of the church is seen by the New Testament as normal, as properly expressive of the true nature of things, as befitting the nature of the relationship between the state and the church. The church saw it not as a withdrawal but as its responsibility for the world. It is a fundamental misunderstanding to believe that the New Testament conception of the state is the fruit of disappointment, disappointment that Jesus was not accepted as the Messiah, disappointment that Jesus did not immediately return to put an end to the history of the world, or disappointment that the crowds in Jerusalem or in Rome did not immediately

18. See Gal 2:19–20.

acclaim Christians as their redeemers. Such explanations overlook the inner unity, essential for the New Testament, between Christ and his church.

One further and still deeper misunderstanding must be identified and rejected at this point. In the discipleship of the Christian congregation, attention must not be centered on a command to become like Christ or to live like him in the sense of a childish and unimaginative imitation. Rather, Christian behavior is rooted in a participation in the nature of Christ. Therefore, those criticisms are out of place that seek to ridicule the concept of discipleship by asking whether we should not imitate Jesus' celibacy, his being a carpenter, or his traveling barefoot as well. The New Testament does not speak of a legalistic mimicking of Christ but of living in him. We are members of his body; we do not become such through discipleship. Discipleship is the expression and not the instrument of our being in the fellowship of Christ. Discipleship is the form of Christian freedom and not a new, harder legalism.

As we said before, it is striking that the concept of discipleship is not applied in a general and formally undiscriminating way in the New Testament. As we have seen above, the apostle Paul was one of those for whom the concept of life in Christ and dying with Christ, with special reference to the sufferings of the disciple, was fundamental. And yet, when this same apostle is arguing that it is preferable for Christians not to marry (1 Corinthians 7), it does not occur to him to base his argument on the fact that Jesus was not married.

Jesus began his early life and his early public ministry in Galilee. His trade as a carpenter, his association with fishermen, and his drawing of illustrations from the life of the sower and the shepherd have, in recent Christian history, given momentum to a glorification of the handicrafts and the rural life. But there is none of this in the New Testament, which is a testimony to the life and witness of a church that intentionally went into the cities in full knowledge of the conflicts that awaited it there. The fact that discipleship is *not* applied by the New Testament at some of those points where Franciscan and romantic devotion has tried most piously to apply it is all the more a demonstration of how fundamental the thought of participation in the suffering of Christ is *when* the New Testament church sees it as guiding and explaining its attitude to the powers of this world.

It was through this understanding of Christ as crucified—into whose crucifixion the disciple enters by becoming a member of his body—that the sixteenth-century Anabaptists rediscovered the dynamic for a christo-logically centered rejection of war. The very first testimony to this position in the sixteenth century is a letter written in the fall of 1524 to Thomas Müntzer, who had just become known as an advocate of revolutionary violence in the service of the Reformation:

> The gospel and its adherents are not to be protected by the sword, nor are they thus to protect themselves . . . True Christian believ-ers are sheep among wolves, sheep for the slaughter; they must be baptized in anguish and affliction, tribulation, persecution, suffering and death; they must be tried with fire, and must reach the fatherland of eternal rest, not by killing their bodily, but by mortifying their spiritual enemies. Neither do they use worldly sword or war, since all killing has ceased with them . . .
>
> The brother of Hujuff writes that thou hast preached against the princes, that they are to be attacked with the fist. Is it true? If thou are willing to defend war . . . or other things which thou dost not find in expressed words of scripture . . . then I admon-ish thee by the common salvation of us all that thou wilt cease therefrom and from all notions of thy own now and hereafter . . . And if thou must suffer for it, thou knowest well that it cannot be otherwise. Christ must suffer still more in his members. But he will strengthen and keep them steadfast to the end.[19]

Here, there is no proof-texting, no Pharisaical idealism, no search for purity through non-involvement, and no vision of a model rural community where no force would be needed. There is only the clear and confident identification with the path of Christ, a path not to be trodden in one's own strength or for one's own justification. "Christ must yet suf-fer more in his members; but he will strengthen and keep them steadfast until the end." For Conrad Grebel, who wrote these lines, the cross was not an inner self-denial as it was for the medieval mystics and for Thomas Müntzer. For Grebel, following Zwingli and to some extent Erasmus, the cross is the way and the faith of Christ in this world. A christocentric ethic is an ethic of the cross.

---

19. See George Hunston Williams and Juan de Valdes, *Spiritual and Anabaptist Writers: Documents Illustrative of the Radical Reformation* (Louisville: Westminster John Knox, 1957) 81, 85.

7. Love and Responsibility

WE HAVE DEVOTED THE previous two lectures specifically to the teaching of the New Testament on the church and war. We have dealt independently with the teachings of Jesus and with his person as the Messiah. Although treated quite independently, we have discovered that the lesson was the same in both cases. But our task is far from fulfilled with these observations on the teaching of the Bible.

Speaking broadly, the position we have described is generally recognized to have been that of the Christian churches of the early centuries. But much has happened since that time. Different practices have developed and quite different reasons for those practices have been offered. Therefore, we must devote the remaining lectures of this series to the most important explanations used (by theologians and laypersons) to justify the serious digression from this New Testament position, a digression that became the predominant Christian position soon after Constantine and has remained so ever since.

Some of those who rejected the early church position did so—and some do so today—because they were not concerned that their decisions should be directed by the commands of the example of Jesus Christ; they honestly believed that the empire or the nation was an absolute value in itself. Others, especially in the age of the Crusades, were convinced that they had a new and particular divine mission to fulfill through war in the name of the church. But our concern here is with the serious thought of those who avoided such simple and un-Christian extremes and who seriously faced the need to come to terms with the demands of the gospel.

In most cases, the processes whereby decisions are made by Christians are inarticulate and not carefully reasoned. Yet, a logic which we will do well to study in the form of its most worthy expressions lies behind these decisions. We shall analyze one expression of a modern mentality (in this chapter) and another from an ancient tradition (in the next).

The most current and contemporary line of thought in the Protestant world of Western Europe and North America is best expressed by Reinhold Niebuhr. It represents the logic of many who are not directly his students and would not use precisely his language. His thought rephrases for our time concepts that go back to the Protestant Reformation—especially to Martin Luther—so that we may take his thought as representative without being unfair. Let us, therefore, seek to display its basic outlines.

A. Professor Niebuhr begins with the ready recognition that Jesus taught nonresistant, suffering, unconditional love. There is in this serious theology no childish effort to exploit the words of John the Baptist to the Roman soldiers, or the cleansing of the temple, or the death of Ananias and Sapphira, as if they proved that not all killing is forbidden by some sort of negative legalism. The duty of absolute love as taught and exemplified by Jesus is not debatable for Professor Niebuhr.

B. But absolute love is also impossible. Jesus taught and lived in the face-to-face society of rural Galilee. He could meaningfully ask his hearers to be absolutely loving, for you can be absolutely unselfish with one person at a time in such a simple society. But we live in a society where such ideals are impossible to apply, not only because of our innate sinfulness but also because of the situation. It is not possible to give one's cloak to a thousand beggars. If our society has taken certain wholesome measures for the rehabilitation of the indigent, it may in fact be harmful to give it to any of them personally.

Jesus taught absolute love within the expectation of an early end to the world and the miraculous establishment of a messianic kingdom. He could teach his disciples to take no thought for the morrow because he would return tomorrow. The imminent promised triumph of the kingdom could be the only source and standard of his moral teaching. Survival was not a concern for the individual or the society. But we know that Jesus and the early church were wrong in this hope. The kingdom did not come with the sending of the twelve disciples, nor at the crucifixion, nor when Paul reached Rome. We have all made our peace—says Professor Niebuhr—with the fact that it never will come in that simple, cataclysmic sense which seemed self-evident in New Testament times. The survival of the social order and the maximum number of relatively good people, therefore, becomes a standard for our obedience as it was not for his.

Jesus taught an ideal morality with no attention to the fact that his hearers were incorrigibly sinful. Such teaching is constantly threatened by Pharisaism, and the early Judaistic church was no exception. Jesus' teaching needed the complement that was provided by Paul's reminder of man's abiding sinfulness in God's abiding grace. We now see that law—even the "higher law" of the Sermon on the Mount—is meant not so much to tell us what we should and can do as to bring us to our knees.

Jesus taught the meaning of love to subject peoples and slaves. The best you could do in that circumstance was to see meaning in suffering. But now we live in democracies where the citizens choose their own government and share responsibility for its actions.

C. For all these reasons and more, Jesus' teaching of absolute love needs to be placed in a larger frame. Love must remain our motive, but our instructions must be changed; for reasons that remain the same, we must now act differently. It is this larger frame that we call responsibility.

We have been entrusted—by God but also by the course of history—with certain duties that are our obligation, our responsibility, to discharge. We learn what these responsibilities are not from Jesus but from the situation. What is called for in the situation (i.e., to assure the survival and the welfare of the social order) is the demand of love. It will mean defending justice rather than suffering injustice, using power effectively in the interest of the common good rather than turning the other cheek.

In the sixteenth century, Martin Luther said this in terms of the concepts of office or vocation. In contemporary Anglo-Saxon thought, the key terms are "justice" and "responsibility." Each of these terms has two aspects.

1. Justice is a vision of true equity, of a perfectly fair order which would give "to each his own."

2. But there is also the actual process of providing justice that is corrupted by the pride and the lusts of people but is still the best we have. Even at its worst, this feeble human justice is better than its abandonment; it is preferable to the chaos that would follow if, like Jesus, Christians were to withdraw from social responsibility.

3. Responsibility is, first of all, a fact imposed upon us by the development of democratic forms of government whether we like it or not.

4. But it is at the same time a duty of love, a debt we have to our neighbor by virtue of our Christian love.

D. Logical Analysis

Whether we speak in the language of the sixteenth century or the twentieth, the logical structure of this position is the same.

1. First of all, it says that the Christian has moral obligations that are derived, both in form and in substance, from something other than Jesus Christ. Formally, they have another source in that we do not find these instructions in Jesus, in the Bible, or in the heart of the piety of the church; we find them by observing the needs of the world. In substance as well, these obligations are different from those of Jesus Christ; they call us not to turn the other cheek but to stand up for our rights, not to bear the cross but (under certain limits) to bear the sword.

   Now whether this fact is a weakness theologically or not depends upon one's own doctrinal insight concerning revelation, other revelations, and natural revelation. It is easiest for the North American liberal theologian or humanist to find this view theologically acceptable. It is the most difficult to make a theological case for this kind of revelation otherwise than from Jesus in those theologies which—in conflict either with the Roman Catholic heritage or with the revelation through history of the "German Christians" of the 1930s—have insisted, to use the language of the Barmen Confession, that "Jesus Christ is the one Word of God which we are to hear and obey."[1]

---

1. See the "Barmen Confession" in Hubert G. Locke, *The Church Confronts the Nazis: Barmen Then and Now* (New York: Edwin Mellen, 1984) 22.

2. If we are responsible, the moral standards by which we should be guided will be those that describe the duties of everyone. In spite of legal disestablishment of the churches, North America is firmly within the tradition of the Christian West at this point. When the moralist meditates about right behavior, he is thinking about that behavior which is possible for everyone to carry out. The standard tests by which a statement about right behavior must be measured in our society are:

   a. Can you ask this of the common person?

   b. If everyone does it, what will become of society?

   c. If the ruler follows it, where will our society be led?

   We need only raise these questions to see that the New Testament church would never have thought of trying to meet such tests. In fact, the apostles would have rejected the entire idea because Christian obedience is a fruit of repentance, regeneration, and illumination, supported by the forgiveness and counsel of the brethren and enabled by the empowerment of the Holy Spirit. None of these resources may be presupposed for society at large.

3. The fundamental concern of the ethic of responsibility is to move history in the right direction. For me to assume the responsibility of choosing between more or less justice, it must be taken for granted that I—the agent for whose actions ethics wants to provide guidance—am at the helm of history. If I do A, then result X will follow. On the other hand, if I do B, then result Z will follow. Since Z is obviously a better outcome than X, I should do B rather than A.

E. A Test Case

Having stated a criticism of this argument in abstract theological form, it may be clearer to face directly the simplest common form it usually takes. I used to think it was an emotional, irrational, and intellectually unworthy argument. But this does not keep it from being representative of the thought of more sophisticated thinkers. So let us not spurn the parable.

Nowhere is the modern assumption that our basic responsibility is to make events come out right more naturally and crudely expressed than in the simple question which seems—to everyone, from board member to seminary professor—to be an adequate and unanswerable refutation of the pacifist position: "What would you do if your family were being attacked?"

I should apologize for taking your time with such an un-theological framing of the issue. Yet, I have discovered in many previous efforts at conversation on a more formal level that the situational test of the hypothetical attacker is, after all, what everyone has in mind. This is, then, our second parenthetical digression.

First of all, to be careful with such a case would mean discovering how far it is from being parallel to the act of war. The person breaking into my home is an individual who is responsible for his actions and, should I harm him, it is at least the responsible person who suffers. No one can say this about the victims of current American bombing in North Vietnam. Furthermore, the attacker is fully aware that what he is doing is prohibited by legislation unquestionably in force in the community of which we are both citizens. Should I presume to use violence against him, this action would be subject to review by legal procedure. Some court having authority above both of us would have to decide, on the basis of legislation that existed before the offense or the defense, whether the self-defense was legitimate. In any case, to deter this attacker I would not threaten or destroy his family or his home.

It must also be clear that to attempt to answer such a question would be to enter the realm of casuistry, a theological discipline that is currently not enjoying a good reputation. To claim to be able to know ahead of time what one would do, or even what would be the available options, is to falsify the nature of moral decision. That there are two and only two choices—one of which would be utter disaster for myself and my family, the other of which would be my killing the attacker—has to be built into the question for it to make any sense at all. The most superficial examination reveals this to be a highly preposterous hypothesis.

But let us grant all the questionable assumptions involved in the posing of this dilemma. Let it be assumed that I am in a situation where it does seem preponderantly probable that someone dear to me would suffer severely if I were not to intervene and that a violent intervention, of which I am fully capable, is very certain to be able to deter such an outcome at the cost of the life of the attacker. Would this always be wrong? Or would it be permissible? Or would it be mandatory?

One of the deceptive features of this hypothetical situation of justified defense is the impression it gives that the basic motivation is one of altruism. The protection of another, of an innocent person, would seem to be a moral obligation to anyone. And yet, as a matter of fact, the reason this example has a strong emotional pull is precisely that this is not its character. I would defend *my* wife or *my* children, according to this argument, not because they are innocent and in need of being defended, but much more precisely because they are *mine*. The argument does not presuppose that I would or should or could have the same sensitivity to other innocent persons who are being attacked. Today, as we meet and trade generalizations about ethical obligations, innocent wives and children are probably being attacked in the name of the freedom of the government of South Vietnam and no one among us suggests that each of these innocents places upon any of us an obligation of defense.

But let us also set aside this kind of flaw in the argument and let us admit that, even on the level of *self-defense*, it may meaningfully be argued that I owe—to myself, to my calling, or to the world—a defense of my life and of those for whom I have a special responsibility.

To subject the options lying before me to careful logical analysis will show that five conceivable types of outcomes can meaningfully be distinguished. To begin with, let us renounce all pretension concerning the ability to calculate the probability or even the possibility of one or the other of these.

1. One possibility has traditionally been labeled as martyrdom. In certain cases, it has been held by the Christian church that the death of a Christian at the hands of the agents of evil (because of her behaving in a Christian way) can become, through no merit of her own, a special kind of witness and a monument to the power of God through which the death of that disciple makes a

greater contribution to the cause of God and to the welfare of the world than her life would have.

2. A second possibility which no logical analysis has any justification for excluding would be that of an unpredictable escape. The attacker might respond to an outstretched hand by dropping his weapon. He might stumble. I might think of a word or gesture to disarm him emotionally or of a stratagem to disarm him physically.

3. A third possibility that classical Christian theology will certainly not permit us to exclude, whatever modern humanity might think, is the category of miracle. We cannot be sure what the apostle meant by assuring his leaders that they were not subjected to any tests in which there would be no way of escape. But certainly all biblical faith has affirmed a providential directing of the affairs of humanity toward that end described as "*good for those who love God.*"[2] Since one of the characteristics of providential deliverance is its not fitting into any predictable pattern, it is impossible to say from a perspective of objectivity or of unbelief whether this category of the miraculous is really distinguishable from the category referred to above as unpredictable, namely, the combination of coincidence and imagination that produces an outcome which, although unforeseeable, can after the fact be explained in causal terms.

4. The fourth logical possibility assumes that the persons posing the question know the outcome to be not only likely but certain: through the brutality of the attacker, suffering or even death which would be contrary to God's will or to the good for us will come upon me and mine. It is to avoid this eventuality that the question assumes the only possible reaction on my part to be . . .

5. the fifth choice, which is to take the life of the one who threatens me on my own authority and in the name of the emergency police powers vested in every citizen by the common law.

---

2. Rom 8:28.

When we stop to think soberly, it strikes us as genuinely preposterous that it should be assumed that only the last two of these five eventualities need to be contemplated seriously. Certainly, the lesson of human history is indisputably that death is not the greatest evil which one can suffer oneself because death, for a reason relating to God's will and way, is a part of his victory over the evil of this world. Certainly, the uniform conviction of classical theology has been that the third category—that of miracle—is a genuine possibility. And if we choose to be too modern to deal with such concepts, then, just as certainly, an informed modern grasp of the complexity of historical causality and a soberly documented awareness of how seldom things have turned out the way people have predicted—especially with a vision to the assumed healthful effects of violence—must at least forbid excluding the second possibility, i.e., that of unpredictability.

It is not merely a debating maneuver when we carefully pick up the logic of this challenge. Moving back from the test case to the logic it represents, we can see clearly what might be called the implicit eschatology of reliance on violence. Instead of leaving the choice among the various alternatives (at least three of which would be *saving* alternatives) to the providence of God and to my own consecrated imagination (and that of my dependents), the question assumes as a matter of fact that it is my moral duty to close off those saving possibilities, thereby choosing one of them which is *sure* to be destructive only because it is less harmful to mine, or more legally justifiable, than the other destructive alternatives.

F. Rethinking the Logic of Contemporary Protestant Thought

Backing away from the particular case, one can state the matter as it applies to the broader question of the moral justification of violence and especially of war: by assuming that it is the business of the Christian to prevent or to bring judgment upon evil, we authorize him to close the door on possibilities of reconciliation and healing. When we take it into our own hands to guarantee that events will turn out in a way that is the least painful to us or the least illegal, we close off the live possibility which obedience to the love of Christ might have let loose in the world.

Let us break the logic into smaller steps:

1. First of all, this approach assumes that I am very accurately and correctly informed about what should happen, about the best possible outcome of a given situation. This knowledge of what direction would be best for history is certainly not shared by the adversary (especially not in time of war) and, in fact, it is usually not shared by the neutral parties either. Yet for the purpose of argument, it must be assumed that I have right information on this matter, so right that it can be my holy duty to impose that result on others. I know what the providence of God desires.

2. It is assumed that I have a full overview of all the causally possible alternatives, knowing exactly what results X or Y will follow from my action A or B. Again, this assumption is indispensable to the argument. As a matter of fact, we have little indication from the sciences of history and human relations to demonstrate that people have any grasp of what the alternative possibilities are. The First World War was to end war; the Second World War was to make the world safe for democracy; the present hostilities in Vietnam are to make peace and self-determination possible. The events of history often belie the assumption that those who were making decisions really knew what the results of their decisions would be. Professor Niebuhr himself has referred to this fact as the "irony of history."

3. It must further be assumed that one is able to dispose of sufficient power to make sure that one can impose one's desire on all the other parties to direct the course of history. Again, this assumption is indispensable to the logic. Yet by definition, this assumption can only be true for one half of the parties in all cases of conflict and, in practice, it is true for even less.

4. It must be assumed that it is so important to move history in the right direction that it becomes right to do wrong. That is to say one must wittingly and willingly commit actions which otherwise would be forbidden for the Christian by the example or the teaching of Christ.

5. All of these assumptions must hold with sufficient clarity and certainty that the responsibility to make things come out right can take precedence over simple Christian obedience. This makes

it clear that what is really at stake is the claim to an alternative revelation.

The responsibility argument assumes, as we saw at the outset, that Jesus taught an unattainable, ideal love which can be of no real guidance in society. This concrete impossibility of the ideal makes it easier to argue that some other source of more realistic truth is needed to guide our action in society. But, contrary to this assumption, it has emerged from our study of the words and the works of Jesus that he was quite aware of the social needs and political hopes of his people. Saving Israel by becoming a military leader was for him not only conceivable but, in fact, his greatest temptation, the temptation that pursued him from the beginning of his public ministry to the end.

Jesus rejected the option of military messianity pressed on him by the tempter in the desert, by the crowds on the seashore, and by the Zealots among the Twelve, *not* because:

1. he was interested only in face-to-face personal relations,

2. he thought the world would not last long enough for a messiah to get anything done,

3. being interested only in a spiritual kingdom, he felt it a waste of concern,

4. he was an irresponsible sectarian leaving to others the really difficult jobs,

but because the use of the sword is irreconcilable with the will of God for humans in society. The rejection of the sword as an instrument inappropriate for the achievement of God's purposes among humans and the acceptance of the cross as the price of unconditional love represents the supreme example of human social *responsibility*. The question of responsibility is the question Jesus answered in Gethsemane.

Our answer to those who argue a duty to be an agent of governmental violence is not that we are more optimistic about society's chances for moral renewal nor about humanity's capacity for unselfishness. The question is one of authority. If Christ is simply a symbol of a person's own needs and weaknesses and if a person properly makes his own choices on the grounds of his understanding of how society should move (giving himself the right to dispose of the lives of others toward that end), then there is no possible further argument because that person has made himself his own judge and his own lord.

But if Jesus unites the career of a suffering servant and the exaltation of the risen Lord at the right hand of God as the early church confessed, then true responsibility is not the effort to gain and use power for the ends one judges to be good. True responsibility cannot be opposed to or separated from the path of him whose assignment was to restore Israel.

The real temptation of good people like us is not the crude, the crass, and the carnal as those traits are defined in Puritanism. The real refined temptation, with which Jesus himself was tried, was that of egocentric altruism, of being oneself the incarnation of a good and righteous cause for which others are to suffer, of stating our self-justification in the form of a duty to others. I do not know what I would do if some insane or criminal brute were to attack my wife or my child. But I do know that what I should do must be defined by what God my Father did when his only begotten Son was being threatened and by what Abraham, that human father in the faith, was ready to sacrifice out of obedience. Abraham could obey, the writer to the Hebrews tells us anachronistically, because he believed in the resurrection. It was *"for the sake of the joy that was set before him"* that Christ himself *"endured the cross."*[3] My readiness to accept that kind of love as my duty is founded not in craving for heroism, in self-confidence, in pious enthusiasm, in masochism, nor in the contemplation of my moral strength, but in confession of the nature of the God who has revealed himself in Jesus Christ. It is founded doctrinally—I should even say dogmatically in the proper sense of that term—in the confession that he who as truly God gave his life at our hands was at one and the same time truly human, the revelation of that true humanity which is God's instrument in the world.

3. Heb 12:2.

8. The Values and Limits of the Just War

WITHOUT DOUBT, THE MOST ancient and respected system of Christian thought concerning the moral problem of war is the concept of the just war. Although it is an ancient concept and, therefore, had its first home within the Catholic tradition, it is also affirmed by the basic statements of Protestant doctrine such as the confessions of Augsburg and Westminster.

In modern times it has become fashionable to raise questions as to whether the doctrine of the just war is still tenable. Such doubts were expressed at the ecumenical conferences in Oxford (1937) and Amsterdam (1948), and have also come to the fore in the recent Second Vatican Council. It is our task to evaluate this set of theological criteria regarding war as guidance toward an understanding of the possibilities for responsible Christian thought about war and peace in our age and not merely as a monument of the past.

The Social and Historical Context of Just War Theory

The just war theory came into general use in the age of Christendom and it is characteristic of that context. Following the fundamental changes in the relationship of church and society for which the name of the Emperor Constantine has become the symbol, it came to be assumed that the Roman Empire (and later, by the same logic, all of Western Europe) was identical in membership with the Christian church. It followed from this that the church felt a responsibility to provide moral guidance to society as a whole—most especially for Christian rulers—and not only to the small number of individuals for whom Christian obedience was a matter of deep personal commitment.

No immediate or adequate guidance in answering this kind of question could be discovered from Jesus himself or elsewhere in the entire New Testament because the New Testament assumes that Christians are a missionary minority and that the wielding of the sword is the concern of unbelieving powers. Therefore, we understand the meaning of just war theory best by examining the implications of the concept of medieval society as a Christian body, *corpus christianum*, and not by beginning with the list of specific standards by which just and unjust wars may be distinguished.

Since all of society had been baptized and was under the teaching influence of the infallible church, we would assume a fundamentally similar set of value judgments and insights concerning the nature of right and wrong among all parties in any discussion of moral issues. We would also be able to take the meaning of justice for granted, a mutual understanding that would be much more difficult to reach if there were a greater variety of cultural backgrounds represented.

Whether the entire area of Christendom was actually governed by one emperor or not (and regardless of the great variations in this respect from the fifth century to the fifteenth), it could always be assumed that the Christian Mediterranean/European world was one moral universe or one great cultural family. In thinking about this society, it was possible to see the following as parallel: (a) police authority within a given government and (b) the judging of litigation between families within a given society. The logic of the just war theory is thus, in one sense, a simple extension of the kind of standards that would be applied by the police or by the civil courts in dealing with conflict within an ordered society. The difference is that the police and the courts are superior to both parties in an ordered society whereas, in war, one of the parties must take justice into his own hands. But even within an ordered society provision is made for such cases of legitimate defense or for the individual citizen's taking upon himself the prerogatives of the policeman in an emergency.

The Intellectual Origins of the Just War Theory

Although the most careful elaborations of this theory have been in the works of the great seventeenth-century theologians and philosophers Vitoria, Suárez, and Grotius, the essence of the theory was already present in the works of Augustine. Yet even he was not really the father of this pattern of thought; he borrowed substantially from his spiritual father Ambrose, who in turn had borrowed from his secular mentor Cicero. Ambrose was a civil administrator before he became a Christian and a bishop. Therefore, it was most understandable that he fell back on the most careful pagan thought available on the subject in the absence of Christian sources of insight for dealing with such questions, having been called upon by the necessities of his teaching office in the church to provide moral insight and criticism to the Emperor Theodosius. This theory is an intellectual edifice whose foundations are what theologians call natural law or reason. It is assumed that Christians and pagans will come to the same conclusions. It is no surprise, because of the attitude of the Roman Catholic Church toward human reason, that medieval Catholicism was able to absorb a great body of pagan moral thought. It is more difficult to understand why Protestant thinkers from the sixteenth century to the present have been willing to take over this body of thought unchanged in spite of their insistence upon the priority or even the unique authority of revelation in Christ.

The Peace Concern of the Medieval Church

We seriously misunderstand the theory of the just war if we understand it to be affirming outright that war in general or any particular war can simply be an act of justice or righteousness. A more precise label would actually be "the justifiable war." This doctrine seems to define which kinds of wars it might be possible to justify within very carefully stated and rigorously applied criteria. It is precisely not assumed that war in general is permissible; the contrary is the case. War within Christendom is to be limited to that small number of cases that can meet a very demanding and logical set of formal requirements.

Thus we see just war theory to have been part of a far-reaching concern of the church in the Middle Ages to pacify her many members. When we take into account the glorification of heroic violence—the heritage both of ancient Rome and of the Germanic tribes—we receive a most overwhelming impression of the peacemaking efforts of the churches. Two social institutions—"The Peace of God" and the "Truce of God"—placed the full moral authority of the church behind limitations on the prosecution of even those kinds of hostilities that were held to be justifiable. In other words, even if one's cause is absolutely righteous, there are certain days of the week and times of the year when there shall be no fighting, when the common people should be permitted to go about their daily business, and when the adversaries should be permitted to bind their wounds. Beyond this, the church insisted upon exemption of the clergy from military obligations. This is to say that a real, one-hundred-percent Christian will not bear arms. Anyone who had shed blood, even in a just war or in legitimate self-defense, was required to make penance for this act before he could be restored to full enjoyment of the sacramental fellowship of the church. This makes it all the more clear that the limited recognition of a possible just war was a concession to the exceptional responsibilities of a limited number of rulers and professional soldiers and by no means the blanket acceptance of war as a moral possibility or of general mobilization or militarism as a permanent social condition.

The Criteria of the Just War

Our purpose in drawing up a list of criteria is not to seek completeness nor to provide a lesson in intellectual history but to ascertain the logic behind these standards. One set of questions that any military undertaking must ask concerns the authority for making war, i.e., the criterion of just authority. War cannot legitimately be waged by a bandit or by a common citizen but only by an agency of government already legitimately existing and exercising sovereignty. This is the kind of question that has had such a telling effect in the recent debates in the United States about the war in Vietnam: in what sense could the Saigon administration claim to be a legitimate government?

The above criterion demonstrates that just war theory is essentially a conservative doctrine. If the government that exists is a democracy, the application of the doctrine will support it. But it will also support a feudal or a communistic government if it legitimately exists already. Where there is a conflict of rival governments or a situation of anarchy, there can be no just war according to the theory. This understanding was later changed to adapt to the movement of secular thought, beginning with John Calvin, in order to provide for certain circumstances under which rebellion against tyranny would be justified. Yet this constituted no essential change in the basically conservative implications of the doctrine. The modern glorification of revolution—almost automatically assumed to be the more righteous cause—would have been just as strange to Huguenot thought as to the theory in its earlier Catholic forms.

A second body of critical questions has to do with the particular offense that is assumed to call for military action: the criterion of just cause or just intention. Is the offense clearly a wrong, consciously undertaken by the offending enemy power, for which there is no other remedy? Have all other possible means of restitution been exhausted? Are the aims of the war clear so that the enemy can purchase peace by surrender without being unconditionally destroyed?

One implication of the concept of the just cause, to which we shall return, is that the cause must be a specific, local, responsible offense that is committed by some particular enemy and which can be corrected by the military action proposed. The criterion of just cause forbids the use of war for ideological purposes, to set right evils of long standing for which no one now present is responsible in particular, or to defend one political system against another on neutral territory. This of course condemns both the use of the southern hemisphere as a testing ground for nuclear devices by the United States and the justification of the Vietnam War as a part of the worldwide battle of the United States against communism.

The third set of standards applies to the weapons used: the criteria of just means. Are the weapons and strategy used able to distinguish between the guilty (combatants) and the innocent (civilians, women, children, and the aged)? Is the damage done proportionate to the evil needing to be corrected? Do the methods used respect the nature of humanity as rational and spiritual creatures? Again, these are some of the criteria used most tellingly by those who have condemned the American operation in Vietnam, an operation in which respect for the civilian community has been rendered practically impossible by the nature of the war being waged.

The Great Deception

When I said at the outset of this paper that just war theory has always been the official position of mainstream Christendom, my reader probably did not object. But, as a matter of fact, this has not been the case in any practical sense. The official teachers of moral standards in the monasteries and the official Protestant creeds present this position most clearly. Yet there is no evidence of its ever having been used seriously as guidance in making political decisions, either by princes in the Middle Ages or by constitutional governments in modern times. We have yet to see a substantial case where (a) a Christian politician rejected a war that was in his or her country's interest to wage because it would not be just, or (b) Christian citizens in great numbers refused to wage a war declared by their government because it failed to meet the standards. At the very most, this doctrine would have served to identify the criteria by which a politician or a soldier was dealt with by his confessor. It has never been applied in the crucial—namely the negative—case as an effective limitation upon the assumption of the politician that political reasons are his or her ultimate standard.

If we really want to understand what went on in the Middle Ages, we should look not at the doctrine of the just war but at the crusade, not at those points where moralists developed a logic of *limiting* warfare in principle as an ideal vision but in the concrete practice where the church actually *called upon* populations and authorities to wield the sword on its behalf. We need to find quite different intellectual and spiritual sources for this phenomenon: the holy war of the Old Testament, the German pagan heritage, or the concept of the nearly divine emperor which Christianity had such difficulty in making more modest when it became the religion of the realm. Once the Middle Ages had permitted war for the sake of theological or ecclesiastical objectives, it was a small matter for the later age of enlightenment and rationalism to give the same sweeping moral approval to the wars that a government would wage for uncritically selfish purposes.

Just War Theory in Our Time

If, in our discussion of the issue of war as a moral crisis, we encounter those who hold, contrary to the original intent of the theory, that wars may simply be considered righteous, then we need not limit our response to the contradiction of the New Testament; we may also remind them that the purpose of this doctrine was to provide standards of moral discrimination in the interest of limiting war. If we encounter those who hold that it is still morally adequate as a doctrine, we need to remind them that it has never been seriously applied. Concessions made in the interest of making the doctrine relevant and applicable for the Christian statesman seem to have been wasted since the statesman does not use these standards anyway. If, however, we encounter those who refuse to apply with honest thoroughness the standards of this theory and who still hold that war need not be forbidden, we can do no better than to call them to take seriously the logic of just war theory. For anyone who is not ready, on the one hand, to join with Jesus Christ and the New Testament church in simply rejecting all war and who, on the other hand, still denies that he gives a blank check to the state (whatever state that may be), the only serious and morally responsible alternative remaining is some kind of careful discrimination between those wars which a Christian could participate in and those which he is morally bound to refuse *before* the crucial decision needs to be made. If those with whom we speak accept this logical obligation and provide some formal and objective recognition to their being just as prepared to disobey in the case of an unjust war as to obey in the other case, then we can take seriously their statement that they do not give a blank check or sell out morally to the state.

The relevance of this kind of question should be clearer with every passing year. Ever since the great crises of our century, it is no longer possible to assume that politicians will generally be rational, fair, and humane; the examples abound of authorities quite ready to call upon their citizens to commit acts of monstrous injustice. Beyond this, the proliferation of the means of mass destruction—intrinsically incapable of being used in a discriminating way that limits the damage in proportion to the offense or in a way that respects the immunity of noncombatants—have led those persons who most honestly accept the just war theory to conclude that there is no modern war which can meet its requirements. While falling far short of the position we have found in the New Testament, this rejection of modern war on the basis of the criteria of just war is a serious mark of moral renewal within contemporary Roman Catholicism and, to a less visible extent, within an ecumenical Protestantism as well.

A similar kind of conclusion must be withdrawn with regard to guerrilla warfare, warfare that will, in all likelihood, increasingly be the form of subnuclear hostilities in our age. It is hard to conceive of a case where the criteria of classical moral theory can be met in: (a) the guerilla's challenge to the legitimacy of the official government, not only morally but geographically, (b) the reluctance of the counter-insurgency forces to dignify their repressive action with a formal declaration of war, and (c) the terror, torture, reprisals, and hostage-taking in a war without a front under which especially the civilian populations suffer.

Whether we reject the concept of the just war as unbiblical in origin and spirit or whether we accept it for purposes of conversation as the only instrument of morally earnest non-pacifist thought, the conclusion for our time is the same: there is no serious argument in our day to justify war as a moral possibility for the obedient Christian. Any room the churches continue to leave for their members' participation in war or its preparation is thus unveiled as a surrender of their moral responsibility before the unqualified, idolatrous demands of the *raison d'état* against which just war theory intended to protect us. The medieval—originally pagan—rationalistic doctrine may thus serve—its origins notwithstanding—as a potent tool of ecumenical conversation in the interest of a Christian peace witness.

9. A Biblical View of History

THUS FAR WE HAVE spoken of the gospel and war from within the perspective and the heritage of European and North American civilization. This civilization has been the origin of most patterns of Christian thought on such a subject and of the major international conflicts of modern times. I trust that this treatment of the deep rootage of our problem in the northern hemisphere has not been inappropriate since Europe is the intellectual homeland of much of Latin America as well. Yet it must be recognized that the problems of war, violence, the army, and politics do have a different form in Latin America from the perspective of a citizen of the United States, France, or Germany.

The involvement of your continent in the two major world wars has been much more limited. While there has been serious international conflict on this continent, it has not had the religious and racial character that aggravates the evils of war in numerous other parts of the world. If one can judge from the outsider's perspective, the place of the military establishment in the daily life of Latin American society is different from what the Pentagon signifies in North America in ways I would hardly be competent to list. Your society differs as well in its widespread and still growing sentiment of need for radical social change, so radical that it is widely assumed that it will necessarily be violent.

These most inexpert observations are intended to point to a limitation of the usefulness of these lectures. Although it is unavoidable that our reporting and our thinking on this matter should be rooted in the heritage of the northern hemisphere, any application of the teaching of scripture and the lessons of history must just as necessarily be further adapted to take account of the ways in which not all the peculiar traits of

European and American Christendom have been transplanted here. Such an adaptation cannot be my responsibility. But, in a concluding lecture, perhaps I should suggest some general perspectives that would take into account those dimensions of a Christian reconciling concern in society that go beyond the specific moral issues of war and the military. The case of warfare best dramatizes the break with habitual ways of thinking that is necessary if the church is to be faithful. Even in Latin American thought, we shall do well to keep this case clearly in mind despite the fact that no Latin American nation is out to conquer the world or to "pacify" Southeast Asia. This radical case is but one of many applications of what the apostle Paul called *"the renewing of your minds"*:[1] the call for a view of the world and of history—a mind—that is not conformed to the surrounding world and its habits of thought but transformed by the contemplation of the mercies of God.

Our task is to suggest what kind of change in our view of the world follows, quite apart from the example of war, if we faithfully adjust our minds to the confession that it is Jesus Christ, the crucified one, who is Lord.

The logical choice and normal temptation that seems to present itself at this time is the path which some call pietism. According to this position, faith in Jesus Christ changes the inner, spiritual, and personal dimensions of our life but does not immediately go any further. The result of this limitation of the effects of Christian commitment is not (as many would seem to think) that it prevents the Christian from being interested or involved in the power struggle of society. It is at this point that much current ecumenical debate is going on: shall the Christian be involved or not? But this is not the question. Christians are and always have been involved in the social struggle wherever they exist. What is wrong is not that they are not present but that what they do in the social realm is often done after the fashion of this world and according to the examples provided by the surrounding society without receiving substantial illumination or judgment from Jesus Christ. Christians have been involved in the social power struggle for a long time . . . but on the wrong side. The effect of limiting the gospel to individual experience is not that society is not made a Christian concern. Rather, the issue is that the way this concern is expressed is not faithful to the teachings of Christ and the purpose of God.

1. Rom 12:2.

What we need is to stop giving Christian approval to social practices that are not worthy of such approbation. We must learn not to fly a Christian flag over society when its patterns and our involvement in it are calculated according to interest and power. It is this, the formal Christian approbation of existing societies, which Christendom has been doing for over sixteen centuries.

Therefore, we must attach ourselves to the problem of rethinking the substance of our social concerns in the light of the lordship of Jesus Christ. Not only *that* we need to be concerned must be argued (which seems to be the main affirmation of many at present), but also *how* we are to be committed is the question. What is the meaning of power? What is the utility of wealth as a tool of social responsibility? The suggestions made here are not meant to constitute a careful theory nor a doctrine of the state. They are merely exploratory theses calculated to provoke fresh and careful thinking among those who are willing to let the triumph of Christ be their guide.

The Sword Is Not the Source of Creativity

For obvious reasons (mostly because of the ease of observation and the accessibility of the facts), the writers of history have for centuries centered their memories and their reports on the violent side of the story. The characters who have been remembered are the rulers. The great events that have dates fixed on the calendar are wars and dynastic changes. Even such a collective concern as social justice is dealt with in terms of legislation or taxation. This gives to us and our school children the impression that history is basically made up of the interrelations of ruling houses, and that their problems are solved on the battlefield. For many, therefore, it follows almost automatically that if a Christian desires to be useful, the Christian should seek to work on the level of political control. Political strength is the prerequisite for usefulness and the primary way of expressing concern for the neighbor.

We have all read about the public slogan of Kwame Nkrumah, "Seek ye first the political kingdom."[2] Many were shocked by Nkrumah's use of the language of scripture because they assumed Jesus was talking about

2. Kwame Nkrumah, *Ghana: The Autobiography of Kwame Nkrumah* (Edinburgh: Thomas Nelson, 1957) 164.

some spiritual kingdom. But, in fact, most serious Christians would agree with Nkrumah that the preeminent way to be helpful to one's neighbor, especially in an age of resurgent nationalism, is to get control of society.

Scholars in the last century have begun to understand that dynastic history is unimportant at many points. Often, quite different considerations make society take the course it does. Karl Marx has taught us all—even the anticommunists—that the history of our society could be much better written as an economic history: the ways in which goods are produced and distributed are socially more important than who is on the throne. Max Weber demonstrated that intellectual or even theological considerations can make a major contribution to the spirit of an age and to political development. Similarly, the geographer can explain how events are really dictated to a great degree by the placement of travel routes, rivers, arable land, and mineral resources.

In a way somewhat comparable to the liberating effect that new perspectives of analysis have brought to the writing of history, might it not be suggested that the conviction of Christ's lordship should also enable us to read the traces of our own past more fully? For example, let us consider the suggestion that it is not true that the person on top of the social pile is powerful. Such a person is very often the prisoner of the intrigues and deals whereby he reached that position and of the consensus he is attempting to maintain. Frequently, the bargains one needed to make to get into office are the very reasons why, once firmly established there, that person is no longer in the position to help those truly in need, for whose sake he sought to achieve power in the first place. Nor is it to be taken for granted—as popular Marxism has tended to do—that if the former system is intolerable, then some new strong person will surely be able to solve those same problems more successfully. The new prince is not necessarily more humane than the predecessor. The Marxist theory that the state will wither away once the outside sources of injustice have been eliminated is certainly not proven. It is not certain that Marxists in government authority are more effectively able to govern in the interest of the population than rulers of other convictions.

Conversely, there are other more useful ways to contribute to the course of society than by attempting to rule. When the history of the Middle Ages is carefully read, we shall increasingly discern this sort of success in Christianizing medieval society was obtained less by the power of princes than by the quiet ministry of the monastic movements in rebuilding the community from the bottom. Similarly, what we now call modern civilization was created not by governmental fiat but by the research of intellectual (and religious) nonconformists studying the ways of the natural world with the curiosity of the disinterested voluntary searcher. Therefore, let us learn to write and read history as the history of the peoples and not of nation-states, to evaluate a civilization by how it treated the poor and the foreigner and how it tilled the soil and not by the success of its armies.

Humanness Is Not Brutality

History books are not alone in preaching a view of humanity according to which physical and political violence is the ultimate test of the value of personal merit. It is also the case in popular poetry and literature all the way from the classical tales of the age of chivalry to the modern morality legends of the western film, the spy story, and the cover story of the successful businessperson in *Time*. What these stories impress deeply upon the soul is not simply a picture of a character but a view of the universe. They tell us we are in a universe where there are, on the one hand, bad guys who are utterly beyond redemption. The bad guy is not evil because we can know that he has wittingly done evil deeds or expressed malevolent intentions but he is bad by definition, by status, because he belongs to the wrong organization or to the wrong race. The only satisfactory results of the conflict with bad guys must be that they be banished or crushed.

On the other hand, there are the good guys. The good guys live and kill just like the others but they are on the right side because of the cause they represent. This guarantees not only that they have the right to lie and to kill but also that they will always win out in the end. Goodness, like evil, is not morally based.

So we have here a picture of the whole moral universe, one that (at least in the United States) has manifestly influenced the national personality and style in international affairs. We can clearly observe this in the history of the last two years:

1. All conflicts are reducible to black and white moral issues: one party is so wrong that it forfeits its right to exist and the other party is so right that it is authorized to do almost anything for its cause.

2. Moral issues are not determined from a personal perspective but on the basis of sides: the party is guilty and worthy of death by virtue of the system or the race to which it belongs.

3. For those who are on the wrong side, even their good deeds are a deceptive façade; for those who are on our side, even the most evil deeds are excusable.

4. The good guy is sure to be successful in deceit and in physical combat; the story always comes out this way.

This legend paints for youth, those who are most ready to learn, a picture of the nature of the moral universe that is fundamentally false. It is not true—from either the biblical or the historical perspective—that the world is divided into two organizations or two societies where one is good and the other is evil. It is not the case—either factually or according to careful logical or biblical analysis—that the good man is generally triumphant in physical or intellectual conflict. It is not true—from the perspectives either of logic or of the Bible—that every possible means can be considered justifiable if it is used toward an end considered desirable.

At this point, modern critical thinking and faith in Jesus Christ will coincide. They join in their condemnation of the self-justifying vision of conflict and humanness being traced by these legends. Once we dare to challenge the accepted picture, then we can discover that violence and deceit represent a particular form of moral weakness (the same parallel relationship to violence and deceit which we here observe was striking in the Sermon on the Mount as well).

Secrecy and deceit are a form of slavery. The United States' experience of the last few years has frequently demonstrated that governmental secret intelligence agencies have been a major source of *mis*information. Jesus says that transparency and humility are tests of truth and that it suffices to say "yes" for yes and "nay" for nay. Social experience confirms the same point. The liar fools himself first.

Likewise, physical or psychological violence is a confession of moral weakness. He who resorts to blows confesses he has no better arguments.

Violence is weak in its local effects and not only in the motivation and the moral resources that it presupposes. Violence can keep out the enemy but cannot build a wholesome society. It can aggress but not defend. It can revolt but not create. It can eliminate a specific abuse but cannot bring social health. If a regime established by violence is to survive, it can only do so by demonstrating its capacity to increase the areas of freedom and of orderly legal process. The one thing you cannot do with bayonets, as the dictum has it, is to sit on them. And yet our legend literature, which makes virtue, personal courage, and success in combat coincide—as they do not in real life—sustains a pagan, pre-Christian confusion of humanness (and particularly manhood) with virility.

If You Wish Peace, Prepare for It

A logical extension of confidence in the sword is the ancient maxim, "if you wish peace, prepare for war." The only kind of peace of which this could be said with any truth was the kind of imperial control that was once called the *Pax Romana*. Once there are several nations instead of one emperor ruling the world, the effect of the armaments race has generally been to precipitate the very wars its advocates (on both sides) claimed they were going to prevent.

The alternative to this self-glorifying identification of peace with the predominant power of one's own nation or class is neither a passive unconcern with the distress of one's fellow human nor is it a utopian expectation about the ability to create a warless world. The alternative is the concentration of Christian attention to the creative construction of loving, nonviolent ways to undermine unjust institutions and to build healthy ones and not to the pragmatic predictability of good results promised by recourse to coercion.

War Is Not a Way to Save a Culture

The natives of North America, when threatened by European invasion, fought back militarily. Even though they had some technical advantages in their knowledge of military methods adapted to the terrain and were able to play the French and British colonizers against each another, the North American natives were defeated. Their few surviving heirs have been demoralized, their culture has been degraded, and their society has been pushed into a rural ghetto.

In contrast to this, the natives of what we now call Latin America, facing invaders who were no more gentlemanly, did not fight back in the same way. The Iberian invaders were able to sweep over the entire continent, spreading themselves thinner because they met less opposition, even from the highly organized societies of Mexico and Peru. As a result of the inability or unreadiness of the natives to defend themselves militarily, their population and many of their cultural values have survived to become an integral part of contemporary Central and South American civilization. From the point of view of the European settlers, permitting the indigenization of Catholic religion was a dubious form of Christianization. But our question from the native side is whether war is a way to preserve one's cultural values. The corruption of Catholicism in Latin America by the absorption of elements of the pagan native heritage is a proof of the cultural wisdom of letting the invader enter and "roll over the top" of one's society instead of fighting him to the death.

The fundamental assumption made by our society is this: although war is regrettable—almost infinitely so—it would be still worse to see our civilization destroyed. Therefore, war becomes ultimately necessary for the sake of civilization which only war can preserve. This is, however, not a statement about moral logic. It is a prediction about the course of political history. Is it actually the case that war is the best way to preserve a society? Is it the case that national sovereignty is the best way to encourage cultural growth?

As long as the Roman Empire was strong enough to repulse the invaders from the north by massive military means, this effort became increasingly ineffective and also corrupted and impoverished the internal life of the Roman Empire. But once the central Roman authorities were no longer in a position to defend their borders, wave after wave of Goths and Franks were permitted, first, to infiltrate into the northern provinces and, second, to roll over all of Western Europe. They conquered so much territory and spread themselves (and their royal families) too thin to administer the entire area. The population over which they moved—and, in fact, most of the social and cultural institutions of that population—were able to survive intact, thus laying the foundation for the emergence of a new society out of the "dark ages." It was because of the weakness of the government of the Roman Empire at the right time that the cultural strength of the Christian-Roman heritage was able to sprout again from the roots, a reemergence that could not happen in those places where there was a brutal battle for every foot of ground and where populations and institutions were destroyed or transplanted.

A third example is suggested by the great historian Arnold Toynbee in *The World and The West*.[3] Turkey and Russia are examples of nations that attempted to respond in kind when threatened by the cultural and military power of Western Europe. They sent their brightest young men to France and Prussia to study in military academies and bring back knowledge of military institutions and techniques which, it was assumed, would permit them to meet the Western Europeans in their own game. But when these young men came back to Russia and Turkey, the social fermentation that they brought about disoriented their peoples psychologically and culturally. The Western military spirit introduced a cultural "foreign body" which these nations were never able to assimilate fully except at the cost of recurrent revolution and disavowal of their own earlier history.

On the other hand, India made no effort to define and defend its identity in western terms. The bright young men who went off to school in London studied not military science but law and philosophy. They led India in a process of cultural development, a much less violent movement toward political independence. This movement was certainly just as effective as the efforts of Turkey and Russia to defend their national identity but with much less inner emotional upheaval. India is still India.

All of these examples may be challenged by the historian. I would not claim that they are more than samples of a mode of thought which, with care and imagination, will discern in concrete cases the relevance of this truth: it is the crucified one who is reigning at the right hand of God and, therefore, violence will ultimately condemn itself.

Social Creativity Is a Minority Function

We have always been taught to understand the nature of power in society like this: the way to get useful things done is to find a place at the command posts of the state and then to use that power to get things done. We

3. See Arnold Toynbee, *The World and the West* (Oxford: Oxford University Press, 1954).

have already suggested that those in power are not as free or as strong as one assumes, that they are prisoners of the friends and the promises they made in order to get in office. But an even more basic observation is that they are not at the place in society where the greatest contribution can be made. The creativity of the "pilot project" or of the critic is more significant for a social change than is the coercive power that generalizes a new idea. Those who are at the top of society are occupied largely with the routine tasks of staying in position and keeping society in balance. The dominant group in any society is the one that provides its judges and lawyers, its teachers and prelates, most of whom work to keep things as they are. This busyness of the rulers with routine gives an exceptional leverage to the creative minority, sometimes because it can tip the scales between two power blocs and sometimes because it can pioneer a new idea. In every rapidly changing society, a disproportionate share of leadership is carried by cultural, racial, and religious minorities.

What is said here about the cultural strength of the numerical and social minority could just as well be said with regard to *political* strength. The freedom of the Christian (or of the church) from needing to invest in one's best effort (or the best effort of the Christian community), first, in obtaining the capacity to coerce others and, second, in exercising and holding on to this power is precisely the key to the creativity of the unique Christian mission in society. The rejection of violence appears to be social withdrawal if we assume that violence is the key to all that happens in society. But the logic shifts if we recognize that the number of locks that can be opened with the key of violence is very limited. The renunciation of coercive violence is the prerequisite to a genuinely creative social responsibility and to the exercise of those kinds of social power that are less self-defeating.

Evangelical Nonconformity

When Jesus said to his disciples, "*The kings of the Gentiles lord it over them; and those in authority over them are called benefactors. But not so with you,*"[4] he was not calling his followers to a legalistic withdrawal from society out of concern for moral purity but to an active missionary presence

---

4. Luke 22:25–26.

within society. This could be a genuine source of healing and creativity because it would take the pattern of his own suffering servanthood.

Jesus thereby unmasks the pretension to use violence for the good as being a form of hypocrisy: these rulers may call themselves "benefactors" but they are not servants. He who would claim to have the right to use violence, and especially legal violence against another, places himself outside of the scope of Jesus' mode of servanthood. It is not so much because he sins against the letter of the law from the Old Testament or the New but because of the intrinsic pride of his claim to have the right—whether on the basis of official status, or superior insight, or of his moral qualities—to determine the destiny of others in a definitive way. The older language in which the theme of "conformity to this world" was stated in biblical times had to do with idols, with those unworthy objects of devotion to whom people sacrificed in their blindness. Therefore, it is quite fitting to describe the use of violence as being the practical outworking of a fundamental idolatry: if I take the life of another, I am in essence saying that I am devoted to some value to which I sacrifice my neighbor, a value other than Jesus Christ or the neighbor herself. I have thereby made an idol of a given nation, social order, social philosophy, or party, to which I am ready to sacrifice not only something of my own but also the lives of my fellow human beings for whom Christ gave his life.

In the deep nonconformity of mind to which the gospel calls us, we cannot accept the analysis according to which one kind of action (i.e., suffering servanthood) is right from the point of view of revelation but some other pattern is equally right from the practical perspective. This is ultimately to deny the lordship of Christ and shut him up in the monastery or in the innermost heart of the individual. There is clearly a double standard in the world: it is not between discipleship and common sense but between obedience and rebellion.

In the world, there will continue to be *"wars and rumors of wars"*[5] and yet our Lord Christ is not thereby shut out of that world. He is able to overrule even its brutality; he is able to make it so that *"human wrath serves only to praise [God]."*[6] The call to those who know he is Lord and who confess him as such is not to follow the fallen world in the kind of

5. Matt 24:6.
6. Ps 76:10.

self-concern which he must overrule but to follow him in the self-giving love by which all the nations will one day be judged.

When John, the seer of the Apocalypse, wept at the news that no one could break the seals and open the scroll to reveal the meaning of history, the angelic gospel was that it was the Lamb that was slain that is worthy and able to open and to reveal, to whom blessing and honor and glory and power shall be given eternally. This is the gospel view of history. This— and neither a dreamer's confidence in the inborn goodness of humanity nor in the omnipotence of technical organization—enables our patience in defeat and our confidence as we follow the way of the cross as the most constructive social strategy for our age.

III. Church in a Revolutionary World

10. The Otherness of the Church

THAT THE CONSTANTINIAN ERA is coming to an end is one of the common assumptions of Western social analysis. The disintegration of the medieval synthesis of religion and society takes one form in northern, post-Protestant Europe and another in Latin Europe. Similarly, its form and rate of decline in Anglo-Saxon and Latin America differs, but this variety hides from no one the fact that the framework of thought about the church, the world, and their mutual interrelations—which for centuries was shared by all mainline Christian theologies, whether Protestant or Catholic, traditional or enlightened—has fallen away in the last two generations. The assumption that we live in a Christian world no longer applies.

Large layers of the population in every modern society—intellectuals, proletarians, and youth—simply bypass the churches that dictated every aspect of life a few generations ago. Often the churches are not even paid the compliment of outright rejection; the men who believe they represent the future find what they understand of the Christian faith to be simply irrelevant.

The predominant theological response to this development has been to face the fact without evaluating it. Apart from the few clericalists and monarchists who are still trying to revive the past, most thinkers simply try to make peace with the new situation as they had with the old, assuming that the total process is God's doing. For the first three centuries Christians were persecuted by the world—that was how it had to be. For over a millennium Christians ruled the world—that was as it should be. In the modern age, the world again faces the church as an autonomous, articulate, partly hostile quantity—that is as it should be. In the sentiments of the patient Job, they accept without understanding and adjust without seeing meaning in events: *"The Lord gave, and the Lord has taken away; blessed be the name of the Lord."*[1] The early church was right in facing persecution; the church of the fourth century was right in making her peace with the world; the churches of the Middle Ages and Reformation were right in leaning on the state; now that this is no longer possible, the church is again right in making the best of a bad deal.

But this is not a theologically acceptable interpretation. We have learned that history reveals as much Antichrist as Christ. We are no longer sure, as some hopeful Christians of two generations ago could be, that we are still edging upwards at the top of a progression of which every preceding step must have been right for its time since it led us to this pinnacle. But, above all, we have learned to ask if it can really be the will of the Lord of history that his church should be limping after history, always attempting to adapt to a new situation that it assumes to be providential, always half a step behind in the effort to conform. Therefore, we cannot say whether the de-Constantinianizing of the church—in the form of disestablishment in East Germany, in that of defecting membership and anticlericalism in Western Europe, or in the more complex forms taken by post-Christendom paganism elsewhere—is a bane or a boon until we have sought a deeper understanding of the roots of modern secularism, of the *Mündigkeit*, of the "coming-of-age" of the world. In this search, we shall attempt to illuminate some old answers with a new question.

The Otherness of the Early Church

We begin by seeking to isolate the concepts "church" and "world" in their pre-Constantinian significance. World (*aion houtos* in Paul, *kosmos* in John) signifies in this connection neither creation, nature, society, humanity, or universe but, rather, the fallen forms of the same which are no longer conformed to the creative intent. The state, which for present purposes may be considered as typical for the world, belongs in this realm with the other powers (*exousiae*). Over against this world, the church is visible and identified by baptism, discipline, morality, and martyrdom. For the early centuries, it is self-evident that the church's members as a

---

1. Job 1:20.

visible fellowship of disciples do not normally belong in the service of the world and, *a fortiori*, in that of the pagan state.

But behind or above this visible dichotomy is a believed unity. All evidence to the contrary notwithstanding, the early church believed that its Lord was also Lord over the world. The explicit paganism of the state, art, economics, and learning in Greece and Rome did not keep the church from confessing their subordination to him who sits at the right hand of God. This belief in Christ's lordship over the powers enabled the church—in and in spite of her distinctness from the world—to speak to the world in God's name, not only in evangelism but in ethical judgment as well. The church could take on a prophetic responsibility for civil ethics (for example, Tertullian) without baptizing the state or the statesman. The justice asked of the government was not Christian righteousness but human *justitia*. This could be demanded from pagans not because of any belief in a universal innate moral sense but because of faith in the Lord. Therefore, the visible distinctness of the church and the world was not an insouciant withdrawn irresponsibility; it was a particular, structurally appropriate way—and the most effective way—to be present and responsible.

This attitude was meaningful for the church because it believed that the state was not the ultimate determinative force in history. The church ascribed to the Roman Empire a preservative function, at best, in the midst of the essentially rebellious world whereas the true sense of history was to be sought elsewhere, namely, in the work of the church. The church's high estimation of its own vocation explains both its visible distinctness and the demands addressed to the world. The depth of its conviction that its own task was the most necessary enabled the church to leave other functions to pagans; faith in Christ's Lordship enabled the church to do so without feeling that it was abandoning the pagans to Satan.

The Constantinian Reversal

The early church saw that church and world were visibly distinct, yet affirmed in faith one Lord over both. This pair of affirmations is what the so-called Constantinian transformation changed. The most pertinent fact about the new state of things after Constantine and Augustine was not that Christians were no longer persecuted and began to be privileged nor that the emperors built churches and presided over ecumenical debates about the Trinity. What matters is that the two sociological realities—church and world—were fused. There was no longer any visible quantity that could be called world. Government, war, economy, art, rhetoric, superstition had all been baptized.

The close logical connection between this change and the emergence of a new theological distinction is not often recognized. It was perfectly clear to people like Augustine that the world had not become Christian through its compulsory baptism. Therefore, the doctrine that the true church is invisible sprang up in order to permit the affirmation that, on some level, the difference between belief and unbelief, i.e., between church and world, still existed. But this distinction has become invisible, like faith itself. Previously, Christians had known as a fact of experience that the church existed but had to believe against appearances that Christ ruled over the world. After Constantine, one knew as a fact of experience that Christ was ruling over the world, but one had to believe against the evidences that there existed a believing church. The order of redemption was subordinated to that of preservation and Christian hope turned inside out.

The practical outworkings of this reversal were unavoidable. Since the church has been filled with people in whom the presuppositions of discipleship (repentance and faith) are absent, the ethical requirements set by the church must be adapted to the achievement level of respectable unbelief. Yet, a more significant reason for moral dilution lies in the other direction. The political authority, who a century earlier would have been proud to insist that his profession was unchristian by nature wants to be told the opposite by the middle of the fourth century. What he does is the same as before, if not worse. Yet since there are no more heathen to do the work—since there are no more confessing heathen—every profession must be declared Christian.[2] This does not mean that each profession is Christianized in its substance, which would mean being concretely changed by becoming an instrument of service to others and obedience to Christ according to the commands of the gospel. In the gospel, there are not easily discerned guides to the exercise of every function in soci-

---

2. Author's parenthetical comment within the text: "(Of course, with Augustine, everyone knows that most of the citizens are not true believers. So, actually, there are heathen—baptized ones—to do the tyrants' work. But unbelief, like the church, has become invisible.)"

ety. Therefore, the norms of pagan reason and habit will be taken over to define the content of Christian love. The autonomy of the state and of the other realms of culture is not brought concretely under the lordship of Christ, which would involve the total revision of form and content. It has been baptized while retaining its former content. An excellent example is Ambrose's rephrasing of Cicero's political ethics from which the doctrine of the just war is derived.

Yet, medieval Catholicism maintained significant elements of otherness in structure and in piety that are generally underestimated. The risk of caricature is great when, under the influence of men like Troeltsch, we speak of the "medieval synthesis" and of a fusion of church and world such that the salt had lost its savor. Whatever was wrong with the basic confusion we have just described, the church in the Middle Ages retained a consciousness of her distinctness from the world. The awareness of the strangeness of God's people in a rebellious world, however distorted and polluted, was preserved by: (a) the higher level of morality asked of the clergy, (b) the international character of the hierarchy, (c) its visibility in opposition to the princes, (d) the gradual moral education of barbarians into monogamy and legality, (e) foreign missions, (f) apocalyptic mysticism, and (g) the moral demands of a Savonarola or a Francis. Will the Reformation unearth and fan these smoldering coals into new flame, or will it bury them for good?

The Reformation Transition

The Reformation began with many insights and initiatives that could have led in another direction. But, between 1522 and 1525, both Martin Luther and Ulrich Zwingli decided to ally their renewal movements with political conservatism, thereby withdrawing the challenge to the Constantinian compromise. The Reformers knew very well of the "fall of the church." They rejected the papacy, curialism, Pelagianism, hagiolatry, and sacramentalism, but they dated this fall in the sixth and seventh centuries. They did not discern that these objectionable features of medieval Catholicism were the logical outworking of the earlier confusion of church and world. Therefore, they retained both the social backbone of the Constantinian alliance (religious glorification of and submission to the princes of this world) and its sacramental expression (the baptism of all infants).

Therefore, a fundamental inconsistency in the work of the Reformers remains. They decided in favor of the Middle Ages. They wanted nothing other than the renewal of the *corpus christianum*. Yet, they were driven, for reasons partly of tactics and partly of principle, to shatter that unity which they had sought to purify and restore. We have already noted that the hierarchy, the higher ethical commitment of the orders and the missionary and international character of the Roman church, had preserved (even though in a distorted form) a residual awareness of the visible otherness of the church. All of these dimensions of specificity were abandoned by the Reformation.

In the face of monasticism, the Reformation affirmed the ethical value of the secular vocation. Through the imprecision of their terms, this affirmation (right in itself) amounted to the claim (which was as wrong as the other was right) that every calling is its own norm. This heightened the autonomy of the realms of culture immeasurably even if unintentionally. Proper behavior in a given vocation is decided by the inherent norms of the vocation itself and not by Christ. These norms are conceived as being stable and reliably known from creation through reason despite the fall. The Reformers did not *intend* to secularize the vocations and declare the order of creation independent of Christ and this is demonstrated by their continued efforts to give instruction to political authorities and their claim that certain professions are unworthy of the Christian (not those of prince, mercenary, and hangman but those of monk, usurer, and prostitute). Nevertheless, the autonomy of state and vocation was furthered by what they said to the extent that even today many German Lutherans will argue that faithfulness to Luther demands that the church let the state be master in its own house.

When the church of the fourth century wished to honor Constantine, it interpreted him in an eschatological light. For Eusebius, the Christian Imperator stood immediately under Christos Pantokrator: the state had entered the realm of redemption. The Reformation, however, placed the state in the realm of creation. Theoretically, this meant decreasing the state's dignity; practically, it meant increasing its autonomy. The prince in the sixteenth century is a Christian—the noblest and most honored member of the church—but the work he does as prince is a purely rational one, finding its norms in the divinely fixed structure of society and not in Christ. It is, as Luther said, a work a reasonable Turk could do as well.

Further, the Reformers did not call on the state abstractly, on the state as such, on the state universal (the Holy Roman Empire), or on the "states properly so-called" but, rather, on the territorial state—on the Elector of Saxony and milords of Zurich—to carry through the Reformation. The territorial state was thereby loosed from the network of imponderable political and ecclesiastical forces and counterforces that, in their complex entirety, had formed the *corpus christianum* and given an immediate, un-equivocal, uncontrollable divine imperative that was subject to no higher earthly authority. Previously, political action in God's name, such as the crusades, had been possible only in the name of the church universal. Now, religiously motivated political struggle, including war, has become possible between Christian peoples.

The conviction that the center of the meaning of history is in the work of the church, a conviction which had been central in the pre-Constantinian church and remained half alive in the Middle Ages, is now expressly rejected. The prince is not only a Christian and not only a prominent Christian, he is now the bishop. Because true faith and the true church are invisible, the only valid aims of faithful effort are those which take the total secular society of a given area as the object of responsibility. The prince wields not only the sword but all other powers as well. The church confesses in deed, and sometimes in word, that the state and not the church has the last word and incarnates the ultimate values of God's work in the world. What is called the church is an administrative branch of the state on the same level with the army or the post office and whose major business is to provide a properly educated and politically reliable pastor in every pulpit. Church discipline is applied by the civil courts and police. It is assumed that there is nothing wrong with this since the true church, being invisible, is not affected.

It cannot be said that this turn of events was desired by the Reformers. Their uniform intention was a renewal of the visible, faithful body of be-lievers. But the forces to which they appealed for support, the implications of the theological expedients to which they resorted to defend their state church reformation against the criticism of the free churches, and the drives for autonomy that exist in the state and every realm of culture were too strong to be controlled once they had been let loose.

In the context in which the Reformers made this decision, there is much that we can understand and even approve of. The Reformers' points of departure—faith in the omnipotent Word which will not return void if it is rightly preached and the awareness of the providential place and relative independence of the secular order—were true in themselves. But they did not succeed in examining the Constantinian synthesis itself. Therefore, their decisions—which in their minds were understandable and conservative—reveal themselves to have been inconsistent and revolutionary in a broader socio-historical perspective. The order of creation in which they placed the state and the vocations could, with a turn of the hand, become the deistic order of nature or the atheistic order of reason without any change in its inner structure. The right of the government to administer the church in the interest of the Reformation could become a right of the state to use the church for its own purposes. There was no court of appeal. The divine obligation of the local state to shatter the superstructure of the Holy Roman Empire could flip over—especially after the wars of religion had discredited the appeal to God—and appear as the absolute *raison d'état*. The same religious validation of one nation's selfishness can move one step further and permit ideological wars between classes in the same society.

Therefore, it was precisely the attempt of the Reformers to maintain the medieval ideal of the religiously unified society and also to combat clericalism by laying claim on the autonomous dynamics of state and vocation which led to the secularization which defines the modern period. To accept the Constantinian synthesis fully is to explode it. The Reformers created modern secularism, not intentionally by glorifying the individual as the liberalism of two generations ago boasted, but unintentionally through the inner contradiction of their conservatism.

Our Contemporary Challenge

The Constantinian approach has thereby shown itself to be incapable—not accidentally but intrinsically—of making visible Christ's lordship over church and world. The attempt to reverse the New Testament relationship of church and world by making faith visible and the Christianization of the world a historic achievement with institutional forms was undertaken in good faith. But it has backfired. Its sole effect was raising the autonomy of unbelief to a higher power. Islam, Marxism, secular humanism, and fascism—all the major adversaries of faith in the West and the strongest in the east—are not nature or culture religions but bastard faiths, all of them indirectly the progeny of Christianity's infidelity, of the spiritual miscegenation involved in trying to make a culture-religion out of faith in Jesus Christ. As religious adversaries in our day, they are more formidable than any of the outright pagan alternatives faced by Paul, Francis Xavier, or David Livingstone. He who has refused to learn from the New Testament now must learn from history: the church's responsibility to and for the world is first and always to be the church. The short-circuited means used to Christianize the world in some easier way than by the gospel have had the effect of dechristianizing the West and demonizing creation.

What then must be the path of the church in our time? We must first of all confess—if we believe it—that the meaning of history lies not in the acquisition and defense of culture and the freedom of the West, not in helping the rest of the world to reach the material ease of technological civilization, not in the aggrandizement of material comforts and political sovereignty, and not even in stopping communism, but in the calling together of "*saints from every tribe and language and people and nation,*"[3] "*a people of his own who are zealous for good deeds.*"[4] The basic theological issue is not between right and left, not between Bultmann and Barth, and not between the sacramental and the prophetic emphases, but between those for whom the church is a reality and those for whom she is the institutional reflection of the conscience, the insights, the self-encouragement, and the self-deification—in short, the religion—of a society.

If we confess the Holy Spirit and the church with the apostles, we must further recognize that unbelief also incarnates itself. The world must return to the place in our theology that God's patience has given it in history. World is neither all nature nor all humanity; it is the structuredness of unbelief. It is not a neutral realm in which good and evil have equal chances nor is it the sum total of everything outside ourselves.

Parenthetically, we should note two matters of terminology which often cause confusion. In current ecumenical literature, much is being said of the world as the arena of Christian mission and responsibility. This is meant as a corrective and criticism of excessive individualism of which, it is said, the Protestant pietist tradition has been guilty. We may return to speak of the shortcomings of pietism later but, for the present, we are

3. Rev 5:9.
4. Titus 2:14.

seeking only to define terms. When world is used to refer broadly to the whole social scene without attention to the identity of "the prince of this world" or to the *ekklesia* which is charged with mission (as is often the case), such thinking is not necessarily wrong. The point which is being made may be quite valid. But it is not using the concept of world with the fullness and precision of biblical insight, and it does not contradict the point we are arguing here.

A second word about words: we have taken the state as typical of the character of the world for several good reasons. But it should not be thought that the limitations of this foreshortened identification disappear. The world is much more than the state. Furthermore, the modern state— insofar as it is made modest by constitutional controls and democratic procedure and insofar as it serves the true welfare of the community—is no longer to be identified simply with the powers of Rom 13:1–7 or the kings of 1 Tim 2:1–6 and 1 Pet 2:11–17.

We must avoid false internalization for which worldliness is just a matter of attitude; we must also avoid false externalization, labeling certain leisure time occupations or a certain social milieu as worldly. But we must still come to recognize that there are actions, decisions, and social procedures[5] which are by their nature—and not solely by an accident of context or motivation—denials of faith in Christ.

To accept the New Testament vision of the church's minority status leads to two conclusions which are scandalous for the modern mind. The first is that Christian ethics is for Christians. Since Augustine, this has been denied; since Augustine, the first criterion of an ethical ideal for laypersons is its generalizability. From Kant's formalizing of this criterion to the modern lay application in questions like "What would happen if we were all pacifists like you?," the universal presumption is that what is right will have to apply as a simple, performable possibility for a whole society. Therefore, the choice is between demanding of everyone: (a) a level of obedience and selflessness which only faith and forgiveness render meaningful (the Puritan alternative), and (b) lowering the requirements for everyone to a level where faith and forgiveness are not needed (the medieval alternative). This dilemma is not part of the historical situation;

---

5. Author's note in text: "(Note to translator: 'institutions' in the sociological sense— ways of doing things.)"

it is an artificial construction springing from a failure to recognize the reality of the world.

The second scandalous conclusion is that there may well be certain functions in a given society—which that society in its unbelief considers necessary and which the unbelief in a sense renders necessary—in which Christians will not be called to participate. In certain societies, it may well be argued that there will have to be military governments, executioners, usurers, legalized divorce, or even legalized prostitution to avoid greater evils. Further, it could be argued that certain societies may require colonialism for the good of the backward peoples, racial discrimination to keep the peace, freedom for personal fortune-building, and exploiting workers or resources in order to speed economic development. There is not always a clear alternative available to expedite society's smoother operation. But it does not follow that committed Christians are called to invest their slim resources of time and originality in competing for those self-aggrandizing functions which are, at best, agencies of conservation. This was self-evident in the early Christian view of the state. That it had to be rejected later becomes less and less self-evident the longer we live and learn.

This view of the church commends itself exegetically and theologically. Contrary to the opposing view, it refuses to accept pragmatic grounds for deciding how Christians should relate themselves to the world. Like the Messiah's cross, it would still be right even if it be proven ineffective. Yet, after saying this, we must not fail to observe that this biblical approach is in fact the most effective. The moral renewal of England in the eighteenth century was the fruit of the Wesleyan revival and not of the Anglican establishment. The Christianization of Germanic Europe in the Middle Ages was not achieved by the state church structure—with an incompetent priest in every village and an incontinent Christian on every throne—but by the orders with their voluntaristic base, demanding discipline, mobility, and selectivity as to tasks which characterize the free church pattern.

Therefore, it is evident that the phrase "responsible society," widely current in ecumenical social thought, is less than sufficiently clear. Does it mean that society is responsible? What does such a personal term as responsible mean when applied to a society? Who carries this responsibility? The government? The population at large? The slogan itself is no help in answering. But if we analyze the entire body of thought being disseminated under this slogan we discern that it amounts to a translation into modern terms of the two ancient axioms: (a) the most effective way for the church to be responsible for society is for it to lose its visible specificity while leavening the lump; and (b) each vocation bears adequately knowable inherent norms in itself. We are invited to repeat the mistake of the Reformation just at the time when the free church vision is most needed; the younger churches—in an essentially pre-Constantinian situation—will be encouraged by this slogan to think not in free church terms appropriate to their context but within the *corpus christianum* framework which has already dechristianized Europe.

Christ's victory over the world is to be dated AD 29 or 30 and not AD 311 or 313. The church that follows him most faithfully in that warfare whose weapons are not carnal but mighty will partake most truly in his triumph. The church will be most effective when it abandons effectiveness and intelligence for the foolish weakness of the cross which contains the wisdom and power of God. The church will be most deeply and lastingly responsible for those in the valley of the shadow if it is the city set on the hill. The true church is the free church.

How then do we face the ending of the era of Constantine? If we, like Job, meet it as just another turn of the inscrutable wheels of providence or just one more chance to state the Constantinian position in new terms, then the judgment which has already begun will sweep us along in the collapse of the culture for which we boast that we are responsible. If we discern only one more challenge to try to regain lost ground and reinstate ourselves as court preachers to the mighty in the new power structures, if we try to establish free-thinking, broad, modern Protestantism in the place just vacated by a Catholicism held to be too traditionalist and narrow, or if we see the churches' loss of pomp and prestige as a dirty trick of some seditious elements we must denounce, then we shall be merely repeating the doomed experiment.

But if we have an ear to hear what the Spirit is saying to the churches, if we free ourselves from the bonds[6] which the theology of the official Reformation placed on Protestant thought by its failure to rediscover the fully evangelical vision of the church as the missionary minority . . .

---

6. Author's note in text: "(Note to translator: mortgage? *hypotheque?*)"

1. If we puncture the myth of a unilinear social evolution irresistibly producing a better and more humane social order by evolution or revolution as needed, which the church need only bless with her collaboration . . .

2. If we see the genuinely minority status of the church in mission, even in the falsely so-called Christian world, as a vocation and not as a handicap . . .

3. If we believe that the free church and not the free world is the primary bearer of God's banner, the fullness of him who fills all in all . . .

4. If we face de-Constantinianization not as just another dirty trick of destiny but as the overdue providential unveiling of a pernicious error . . .

. . . then it may be given to us, even in the twentieth century, to be the church. For what more could we ask?

11. Christ and the Powers

As Christians, and especially as evangelical Christians, we desire to let all our thought be guided by the Bible. Even with this intention, we find ourselves facing two major difficulties when we come to speak of the place of the church in the world and the attitude of Christians with regard to the movements of history.

On the one hand, we clearly seem to see realities of which the Bible cannot speak in the world around us. The New Testament was written over a period of a very few years by persons who had no immediate contact with or responsibility for the great political and economic movements of history. Therefore, we find no direct attention to the kind of questions that modern humanity deals with under the heading of "the philosophy of history" or "the philosophy of culture" in the New Testament. The concept of progress is fundamental to a modern understanding of a person's place in the universe. History is understood as the rising and falling of civilizations. The most striking development in history that concerns us is the creation and obsolescence of that magnificent cultural synthesis we have called Christendom. How could we expect the Bible, and especially the New Testament where what we call the gospel is finally stated, to provide us with any assistance in evaluating the flow of history or any guidance in making our contribution to it as responsible Christians?

Another way of characterizing the modern view of reality is to say that we think in terms of structures and institutions. Society is described as a complex set of interweaving customs, traditions, organizations, racial and economic groupings, schools of thought, and the like. Again, the New Testament was written by individuals carrying little or no responsibility for the structures of their society. Some of the early Christians were landowners but, apart from those of their number who sold their property, we know nothing of what they thought about the landholding patterns of their society. Some of them were craftsmen. Yet we know nothing about their thought about how to regulate a market economy. Some of them were slaves, and all we know of their social thought is that they did not revolt. Some persons in minor governmental authority were spoken to by the gospel, but we have no record of whether or how many of them continued to make a Christian contribution in that context. Therefore, it seems that whether we speak of the perspective of historical development or of the structural analysis of modern societies, this is an area to which the gospel would have little to say.

The other basic embarrassment in the effort to relate the Bible to our times is the presence—even in the most intellectually careful portions of the New Testament—of language for which modern humans have no use. On first reading the New Testament writers, one gets the impression that the universe was haunted by various and sundry unseen powers acting behind the scenes to determine the course of events. The essence of the modern scientific worldview, we have been told, is that it limits its attention to visible causes and empirical effects. Human intellectual progress in a reasonable understanding of the world occurs to the extent that people cease to believe that events are in the control of spooks and fairies. After overcoming the ancient idea of spirits behind visible events, people, first, overcame their fear of studying these events and, second, they discovered the natural laws that really do govern them. Science, and thereby the modern world, is characterized by overcoming superstition and limiting our concern to the realities we can see. Therefore, it is no surprise that those portions of the New Testament with which we can do the least are the places where, especially in some of the writings of the apostle Paul, we read of principalities and powers, thrones, archangels, dominions, and the like.[1]

Observing, on the one hand, the problems to which the Bible does not speak and, on the other, the language of the New Testament that seems irrelevant, it is no surprise that Christians at large (and especially Protestants) have often come to the conclusion that the realm of church and society or "Christianity and history" is the one in which we should expect the most common terrain to unite the Christian and non-Christian.

1. See Eph 6:12.

Or, stated negatively, this is the realm where we should expect Christian commitment to make the least difference. Therefore, Protestants have been quite able and ready to borrow extensively from the ideas of non-Christians in this realm. The ideals of liberty, democracy, progress, and social justice have been taken over without much question from those who used the same words outside the Christian fellowship. If Christians contribute anything of their own to defining these goals, it is assumed this would hardly happen in a radical way or in a way that brings them to fundamentally different conclusions about the meaning of the good life for humans.

Christ and the Powers in Current Theology

One significant step forward in theological research in our day has been the discovery that these two difficulties are actually deeply related. With proper analysis, what dismays us at one point turns out to be the answer we need at the other.

Driven by the events that shook Europe between 1930 and 1950, Protestants sought a deeper theological understanding of the power of evil they had seen unleashed in that most civilized of societies. No longer ready to assume that humanity and its institutions can solve their problems, they began to ask again what their confession of Jesus Christ might say to their society's distress. At the same time, equipped with the tools of modern scholarship (which have given theologians in our day a better capacity to understand the meaning of scripture in its initial historical setting—better than has ever been possible since the end of the apostolic age), some theologians have successfully renewed the effort to understand the meaning of precisely those portions of the New Testament that had been the least clear or least "rewarding" before. For instance, they have not attempted to evaluate the writings of the apostle Paul according to whether he sees the world exactly as moderns do. Rather, they have learned to ask what the apostle was intending to say—speaking in and to his own world with its own language—when he used concepts that are no longer self-evident in their meaning for us.

By the providence of God, these two searches led to a common result. It has been discovered that Paul, in his reference to the powers,[2] was using

2. Author's note in text: "(For our purposes we shall use this common designation although his vocabulary was much richer.)"

this term to express a general view of the structuredness of the world and its place in God's purposes. The part of the gospel that we were not able to read before speaks directly to the questions for which we thought the gospel had no answer before.

Although this kind of research has been widespread in European theology the last twenty years, I rely, with special gratitude, on the transparent synthesis provided by Hendrik Berkhof—historian, educator, and member of the Executive Committee of the Central Committee of the World Council of Churches—who has drawn together a synthesis of the meaning for today of the message of the apostle Paul in the smallest compass.

The Origin of the Powers in the Creative Purpose of God

> *He is the image of the invisible God, the firstborn of all creation; for in him all things in heaven and on earth were created, things visible and invisible, whether thrones or dominions or rulers or powers—all things have been created through him and for him. He himself is before all things, and in him all things hold together.*[3]

The word that we translate *"in him all things hold together"* (v. 17) has the same root as the modern word "system." This, the apostle Paul affirms—John would speak of the preexistent Logos—is the part of Christ in creation; it is in him that all "systematizes," that all hangs together. That *whole* that Christ holds together is the world of the powers. It is the realm of creaturely order whose orderliness, in its original intent, is a divine gift. Most of the New Testament references to the powers deal with them as fallen. It is important to begin with the recognition that they were part of God's good creation. Society, history, and even nature would be impossible without regularity, pattern, and order. God has met this need. The universe is not sustained immediately and erratically by an unbroken chain of new divine interventions; it was made orderly and that was good. The creative purpose operates in a mediated way, through the powers that undergird and regularize all visible reality.

---

3. Col 1:15–17.

The Fallen Powers in the Providence of God

Yet we do not find God's good creation before us. Humanity and its world are fallen, and in this the powers have their share. They no longer serve to mediate the wholesome creative purpose. Now we find them seeking to separate us from the love of God (Rom 8:38); we find them ruling the lives of those who live outside the love of God (Eph 2:2); we find them keeping people in servitude to their regulations (Col 2:20–23); we find them holding people in tutelage (Gal 4:3). Those structures that were meant to be our servants have become our masters.

Yet even in this fallen rebellious state, the work of the powers is not merely or sweepingly destructive. They continue to exercise an ordering function even when fallen. Even tyranny—which according to Romans 13:1 falls among the powers—is still better than chaos and we should submit to it. The law—which according to Gal 4:5 can keep humans from becoming mature adopted children—is still just and good and should be obeyed. Even pagan and primitive social and religious forms, though clearly not worthy of our imitation, are a sign of God's preserving patience for the world which has not yet heard the news of his redemption (Acts 17:22–28). Before coming to a portrayal of the work of Christ, Paul makes three basic statements about the structures of creaturely existence in the imagery of his time:

1. These structures were created good. It is the divine purpose that there should be a network of patterns and regularities within human existence which provide the canvass on which the painting of life can be supported.

2. These powers have rebelled or fallen. They have not accepted the modesty required to fit within the divine purpose but have claimed absolute value. They have made people and history their slaves. Humanity is bound under them. In fact, bondage has become one of the most basic New Testament words for the lost condition of humanity outside of Christ. To what are they bound? Humans are bound precisely to the values and structures that are necessary for the life of society but which have taken on idolatrous claims and brought humans to serve them as absolutes.

3. Yet, in spite of this fallenness, the powers cannot escape from the providential overruling of God and he can still use them for good.

Before continuing this discussion of structures and values, let us follow Berkhof in suggesting some of the concrete modern phenomena which he feels are formally equivalent to the powers. At one point he lists "human traditions, the course of earthly life as conditioned by the heavenly bodies, morality, fixed religious and ethical rules, the administration of justice and the ordering of the state."[4] Another list he offers contains: "the state, politics, class, social struggle, national interests, public opinion, accepted morality, the ideas of decency, humanity, democracy."[5] And he continues: the place of the clan or tribe among primitive peoples, respect for ancestors in Chinese life, the astrological unity of ancient Babel, the manifold moral traditions and codes of which moral life is full, the powers of race, class, state, and *Volk*.[6]

If we attempted to analyze this wealth of allusions more abstractly, we could say that we have an inclusive vision of religious structures (especially the religious underpinnings of ancient and primitive stable societies), intellectual structures (-ologies and -isms), moral structures (codes and mores), and political structures (the tyrant, the marketplace, the school, the courtroom, the race, and the nation). The panoply is astoundingly broad and yet, with careful analysis, we discover that it is possible to say just what the apostle has been saying about the powers of all of these realms:

1. All of these structures can be conceived of as, in original essence, a part of a good creation. There could be no society or history and there could be no humans without religious, intellectual, moral, and social structures above them. These structures are not and never have been simply aggregates of individuals. The whole is more than the sum of its parts, and that "more" is an invisible power—though we would hesitate to speak of it in personalistic or angelic terms.

2. Yet these structures fail to serve people as they should in enabling them to live a genuinely free and human and loving life. They are

4. Berkhof, *Christ and the Powers*, trans. John Howard Yoder (Scottdale, PA: Herald, 1962) 29.

5. Ibid., 32.

6. Ibid., 34–35.

absolutized by laying on the individual and on society their claim to unqualified allegiance, thereby enslaving them. Seen from the inside, it is not possible to conceive how people, once committed without qualification to the claims of these powers upon them, could ever be made free again.

3. Yet even though humanity is lost in the modern world, in its structures and the stream of its evolution, it is still within this world that one has been preserved to be oneself and to look forward to a redeeming work of God. One's lostness and survival are inseparable.

Therefore, far from being archaic and meaningless, the *exousiology* of the apostle—his doctrine of the powers—is shown to be a more refined analysis of the problems of society in history than most of the other ways in which theologians have sought to describe the same realities. Some traditional theologies have spoken to this topic under the heading "orders of creation." But it has seldom been possible, under that heading, to combine the recognition of creatureliness, fallenness, and continuing providential control with this clarity and precision. Further, traditional thought about the orders of creation has rarely included religion and ideology. Finally, it has not generally been claimed that it is in *Christ* that all of these values cohere. As a matter of fact, the theology of orders has often claimed that Jesus has nothing to do with them and that the various realms of society are morally autonomous by virtue of their having been created *by the Father*.

Christ and the Powers

If humanity's lostness consists in its being subservient to the rebellious powers of the fallen world, what then is the work of Christ? It is subordination to these powers that make us human. If the powers did not exist, there would be no history, no society, and no humanity. If God is to save us *in our humanity*, the powers cannot be simply destroyed or swept aside. Yet their sovereignty must be broken. Jesus does this concretely and historically by living a genuinely human, free existence among us. This life led him, as genuine human existence leads us, to the cross. In his death, the powers—namely, the most powerfully representative powers of Jewish religion and Roman politics—connived. Like all of us, he was subject to them: he accepted the human state of submission. Yet, morally, he broke their rule by refusing to support the powers in their self glorification. This is why they killed him. Preaching and embodying a righteousness greater than that of the Pharisees and a vision of orderly human social relations more universal than the *Pax Romana*, he suffered the Jews to defile a feast day (thus refuting their own moral claims) and the Romans to forsake legality so that they might together avert the threat to their sovereignty which was represented by his merely *being* in their midst as one morally independent of their claims. Because he did not even fear death, his cross is his victory, the confirmation of his freedom from the rebellious drives of creaturehood. Unlike Adam, unlike Lucifer, unlike all the powers, Jesus *"did not regard equality with God as something to be exploited."*[7] His very obedience unto death is in itself not only the *sign* but also the *firstfruits* of restored, authentic humanity. Here, for the first time, we find a man who is not the slave of any power, of any law or custom, community or institution, value or theory. He would not be their slave even to save his life. This authentic humanity cost him his life at their hands. So it is his death which proves his victory: *"Therefore God also highly exalted him and gave him the name that is above every name . . . and every tongue should confess that Jesus Christ is Lord, to the glory of God the Father."*[8]

> And when you were dead in trespasses and the uncircumcision of your flesh, God made you alive together with him, when he forgave us all our trespasses, erasing the record that stood against us with its legal demands. He set this aside, nailing it to the cross. He disarmed the rulers and authorities and made a public example of them, triumphing over them in it.[9]

The apostle uses three complementary verbs to describe what Christ and his death did to the powers. The way in which these three terms fit together is masterfully condensed in Berkhof's words:

> By the cross (which must always, here as elsewhere, be seen as a unit with the resurrection) Christ abolished the slavery that, as a result of sin, lay over our existence as a menace and an accusation. On the cross He "disarmed" the Powers, "made a public example of them and thereby triumphed over them." Paul uses three different

7. Phil 2:6.
8. Phil 2:9–11.
9. Col 2:13–15.

verbs to express more adequately what happened to the Powers at the cross.

He "made a public example of them." It is precisely in the crucifixion that the true nature of the Powers has come to light. Previously they were accepted as the most basic and ultimate realities, as the gods of the world. Never had it been perceived, nor could it have been perceived, that this belief was founded on deception. Now that the true God appears on earth in Christ, it becomes apparent that the Powers are inimical to Him, acting not as His instruments but as His adversaries. The Scribes, representatives of the Jewish law, far from receiving gratefully Him who came in the name of the God of the law, crucified Him in the name of the temple. The Pharisees, personifying piety, crucified Him in the name of piety. Pilate, representing Roman justice and law, shows what these are worth when called upon to do justice to the Truth Himself. Obviously, "none of the rulers of this age," who let themselves be worshipped as divinities, understood God's wisdom, "for had they known, they would not have crucified the Lord of glory" (1 Corinthians 2:8). Now they are unmasked as false gods by their encounter with very God; they are made a public spectacle.

Thus Christ has "triumphed over them." The unmasking is actually already their defeat. Yet this is only visible to men when they know that God Himself had appeared on earth in Christ. Therefore we must think of the resurrection as well as of the cross. The resurrection manifests what was already accomplished at the cross: that in Christ God has challenged the Powers, has penetrated into their territory, and has displayed that He is stronger than they.

The concrete evidence of this triumph is that at the cross Christ has "disarmed" the powers. The weapon from which they heretofore derived their strength is struck out of their hands. This weapon was the power of illusion, their ability to convince men that they were the divine regents of the world, ultimate certainty and ultimate direction, ultimate happiness and the ultimate duty for small, dependent humanity. Since Christ we know that this is illusion. We are called to a higher destiny; we have higher orders to follow and we stand under a greater Protector. No Powers can separate us from God's love in Christ. Unmasked, revealed in their true nature, they have lost their mighty grip on men. The cross has disarmed them; wherever it is preached, the unmasking and the disarming of the Powers takes place.[10]

10. Berkhof, *Christ and the Powers*, 37–39.

The Powers and Christian Proclamation

If this victory over the powers was the work of Christ, then it must also be the message of the church:

> *Although I am the very least of all the saints, this grace was given to me to bring to the Gentiles the news of the boundless riches of Christ, and to make everyone see what is the plan of the mystery hidden for ages in God who created all things; so that through the church the wisdom of God in its rich variety might now be made known to the rulers and authorities in the heavenly places. This was in accordance with the eternal purpose that he has carried out in Christ Jesus our Lord.*[11]

Again, I cannot improve upon Berkhof's summary:

> Paul's statement is made in connection with the truth that since Christ a new force has made its entry on the stage of salvation history: the church. She is something quite different from Israel as God's people. She is an undreamed-of synthesis of the two sorts of men who people the world, Jews and Gentiles. That Christ has brought both together into one body is the mystery, which for ages had remained hidden (verse 9) but has come to light, thanks to Paul's ministry. In this ministry are manifested "the unsearchable wealth of Christ" (verse 8) and the "manifold wisdom of God" (verse 10).
>
> This is what the church announces to the Powers. The very existence of the church, in which Gentiles and Jews, who heretofore walked according to the *stoicheia* of the world, live together in Christ's fellowship, is itself a proclamation, a sign, a token to the Powers that their unbroken dominion has come to an end. Thus even this text says nothing of a positive or aggressive approach to the Powers. Such an approach is superfluous because the very presence of the church in a world ruled by the Powers is a superlatively positive and aggressive fact. We have already dealt with what this fact means to the Powers, for whom it is a sign of the end time, of their incipient encirclement and their imminent defeat.
>
> This same fact is also freighted with meaning for the Christian. All resistance and every attack against the gods of this age will be unfruitful, unless the church herself *is* resistance and attack, unless she demonstrates in her life and fellowship how men can live freed from the Powers. We can only preach the manifold wisdom of God to Mammon if our life displays that we are joyfully freed from

11. Eph 3:8–11.

his clutches. To reject nationalism we must begin by no longer recognizing in our own bosoms any difference between peoples. We shall only resist social injustice and the disintegration of community if justice and mercy prevail in our own common life and social differences have lost their power to divide. Clairvoyant and warning words and deeds aimed at state or nation are meaningful only in so far as they spring from a church whose inner life is itself her proclamation of God's manifold wisdom to the "Powers in the air."[12]

Therefore, it is a radical misunderstanding to conceive of the social posture of the New Testament church as withdrawal or to see its motivation in the weakness of small numbers, in the fear of persecution, or in scrupulous concern for remaining unspotted by the world. What in our first lecture we called "the otherness of the church" is rooted in its strength and not its weakness, in its being a herald of liberation and not a community of slaves. It is not a detour, waiting for more favorable days to come centuries later, but the church is victorious when it rejects the shortcuts of Zealot and Maccabean patriotism or of Herodian collaboration. The church accepts it as a gift that it is the new humanity created by the cross and not the sword.

This is not to say that Paul is ignorant of a more direct encounter between the faithful and the Powers. Ephesians 6:10–18 proves the contrary. The believer strives ultimately not against tangible men and objects ("flesh and blood," verse 12), but against the Powers they obey. This war with the Powers must be waged seriously. A man must arm himself for it. The arms named (truth, righteousness, the readiness of the gospel of peace, faith, salvation, and the Word of God) show that Paul is not contemplating an offensive against the Powers. Though surely the believer must assure his defense against them, he can do this only by standing, simply, by his faith. He is not called to do more than he can do by simply believing. His duty is not to bring the Powers to their knees. This is Jesus Christ's own task. He has taken care of this thus far and will continue to do so.

We are responsible for the defense, just because He takes care of the offense. Ours it is to hold the Powers, their seduction and their enslavement, at a distance, "to be able to stand against the wiles of the devil" (verse 11, cf. 13). The figurative allusion to weapons points to this defensive role. Girdle, breastplate, shoes,

12. Berkhof, *Christ and the Powers*, 50–51.

shield, helmet, and sword (*machaira*, the short sword) are all defensive arms. Lance, spear, bow and arrow are not named. They
are not needed; these are the weapons Christ Himself bears. Our
weapon is to stay close by Him and thus to remain out of the reach
of the drawing power of the Powers.[13]

This Pauline vision will have crucial implications in current ecumenical discussion about the place of the church in a rapidly changing world.
The preparatory documents for the Amsterdam assembly of 1948, from
which the phrase "responsible society" was drawn, included a pointed insistence upon the necessity for the church to be the church first of all—we
might just as appropriately say "to be the new society"—if it is to have a
ministry to society at large. For example, the church has something to say
to the surrounding society about how racial and economic difference are
dealt with only if the church is a kind of humanity in which racial and
economic differences are overcome.

The basic position paper from which the title "responsible society" is
taken was drafted by J. H. Oldham and it began discussion of "the practice
of communal living" with the statement that "The world cannot be set
right from the top but only from the bottom upwards. There is no way
of restoring substance and depth to the life of man except by living."[14] It
continued:

> The Church is concerned with the primary task of re-creating a
> true social life in two ways. In the first place, its greatest contri-
> bution to the renewal of society is through the fulfillment of its
> primary functions of preaching the Word and through its life as
> a worshipping community. It is the worship of God that is the
> source of all genuine renewal. It is only from His fullness that the
> impoverished human spirit can receive fresh life. It is only in re-
> sponse to the demands of His perfection that it can reach out to
> new tasks. It is His grace and truth that in the last resort guarantee
> and sustain the personal and cultural values that are essential to
> the health of society.
>
> There is nothing greater that the Church can do for society
> than to be a centre in which small groups of persons are together
> entering into this experience of renewal and giving each other mu-
> tual support in Christian living and action in secular spheres. Such

13. Ibid., 51–52.

14. J. H. Oldham, "A Responsible Society," in *The Church and the Disorder of Society:
An Ecumenical Study* (New York: Harper, 1948) 121.

> groups will find their vital inspiration in Word and Sacrament and
> in the fellowship of such gatherings as the parish meeting.[15]

Although the centrality of the church has continued to be affirmed clearly in the basic statements of ecumenical social strategy, it has not been equally visible as the study processes regarding specific social issues have been carried out. These concrete studies needed to relate to problems of social organization about which it often seemed that there was no specifically Christian viewpoint but only correct expert opinion. This opinion is assumed as a basis of collaboration between Christians and non-Christians in the attaining of common social goals and it is not necessarily found only in the church. We cannot be sure that all of this study process has maintained the central importance of the Christian community as new humanity, not only as a doctrine but as an instrument of social change. In the published materials arising out of ecumenical conversation on social ethics, we have been rather successful in avoiding the temptation of the Pharisee: one currently finds little inclination to solve problems with confidence in an unchanging law. One cannot be sure that there has been equal success in discerning and avoiding the temptation of the Sadducees (which is also a servitude to the powers): the belief that the really determining forces of history are in the hands of the rulers of the armies and the marketplaces. Therefore, if Christians are to contribute to the renewal of society, they must seek—among others and in fact competitively with others—to become rulers in the state and the economy in their turn.

Let us avoid two misunderstandings of this critical statement to which we have been driven by the apostle Paul. The point is not, as certain socially conservative religious groups would say, that (a) the gospel deals only with personal ethics and not with social structures, or (b) that the only way it deals with social structures is by changing the heart of the man in power and permitting him to exercise his control with greater humility or insight. Rather, the point is that the primary social structure through which the gospel works to change other structures is the Christian community. In this context, individuals are made humble not simply by a proclamation addressed to their sense of guilt but also by actual social

15. Ibid., 121–22.

fellowshipping with other persons who ask them about their obedience, who (in the words of Jesus) "bind and loose."

The point being made here is not the extreme application of a radical ethical commitment, i.e., the argument that concern with the structures of this world is impure or unworthy solely because of the place of coercion or violence in the governing of society. There might well be points at which the Christian would refuse certain positions in society in order to be morally faithful. Every known ethical system draws some such lines. But if the disciple of Jesus Christ refuses to wield certain kinds of power, it is not simply because they are powerful—for the powers are God's good creation—but because in the given context the rebelliousness of a given power structure is so incorrigible that one's way of taking responsibility for the present most effectively is the path not of collaboration but of objection, not withdrawal from society but negative insertion in the process of social change through the refusal to use unworthy means even for a good end.

It has often been the case that the faithfulness of the church is tested at that point where it is asked to take the path of costly conscientious objection in the face of the world's open opposition. Yet the normal expression of the church's mission in and to society need not be overly dramatized. Its calling is to be conscience and servant within human society. The church should be sufficiently conversant with the ways of this world to be able to discern when and where God is using the powers—whether by means of the faithful testimony of the church or in spite of her unfaithfulness—to contribute to the creation of social structures more worthy of humanity. Yet, the church should also be sufficiently familiar with the manifest ways of God as he has acted in calling together a people of his own so that it will not fall prey to the Sadducean or "German-Christian" temptation of reading a simple statement of his will off the surface of history. God is at work in the world, and it is a task of the church to know how he is working. It should be the first, however, to be able to distinguish between that divine work—which can only ultimately and faithfully be discerned by the light of faith—and the comings and goings on the face of current events of which many people, even many of the church, will be moved to cry out, "lo here!" or "behold there is the Christ!" This task of discernment is far less simple than it has been made out to be by some who have been encouraging us to see God at work in world revolution in the last decade.

It is commonplace that the Christian view of humanity, as fallen yet redeemable, provides a more correct and promising point of departure for looking at society than either the utopian view, which sees it as almost ready to complete its self-redemption, or the mechanistic view, which sees it as a creature of its circumstances. It is even more profoundly true that the biblical conception of the powers in history may provide us with the most adequate intellectual framework for this task of discernment to which we are called in our age. This discernment is not simply a way to help needy people with social problems (a kind of modern day philanthropy) nor is it a guide for individual Christians to help them do right and avoid sin. The church, as no one else can, should proclaim to the powers the fulfillment of the mysterious purposes of God accomplished through that man in whom their rebellion has been broken and the walls they had built have been breached. This proclamation of the lordship of Christ is neither a substitute for nor a prerequisite to the gospel addressed to individuals. It is not a mere consequence of the conversion of individuals in society. These are the two alternatives which previous Protestant thought seems to set before us. But the New Testament does not begin with that dilemma and neither should we. The fact that Christ is Lord, a proclamation to which only individuals can respond, is nevertheless a fact that challenges the powers as well. Therefore, its proclamation is not limited to those who have accepted. Its judgment is not relevant only to those who have chosen to listen. In the words of Johann Christoph Blumhardt, who rediscovered both the miraculous power of the gospel in individual lives and the eschatological foundation of a Christian involvement in politics for German Protestantism: That Jesus is victor is eternally settled: all the world is his![16] This is not a statement about the readiness of people to listen or of the powers to submit. It is a statement about the nature of the universe and the meaning of history within which both our conscientious participation and our conscientious objection have their command and their promise.

---

16. See Christoph Blumhardt, *Jesus Is the Victor* (Farmington, PA: Plough, 2007) 1: "Jesus is the victorious King who o'er all his foes has conquered; Jesus, soon the world will fall at his feet, by love o'erpowered."

12. Constantinianism Old and New

IN AN EARLIER LECTURE, we observed that it is possible to understand the course of Western history as a debate about the relationship between the church and the world. We also saw that the New Testament understanding of the principalities and powers of the present age provides us with a basis for understanding the distinctiveness of the church and a conception of the victory of Jesus Christ which, at the same time, is different from what this world understands by "victory" and yet relates directly to the pride and power of this world. Next we must ask how the Christian church in this age can remain vigilant and sure of its calling.

To begin with, let us continue the story as we found it summarized by Berkhof as he moved from biblical thought to the present with his understanding of Christ's victory over the powers. It is striking to note that, whether by conscious planning or simply because it seemed natural, Berkhof does *not* provide a rationale for a Constantinian union of the church and world. His application of New Testament insight leaps over the Middle Ages and finds its best illustration in the missionary enterprise of recent centuries which understands that the proclamation of the victory of Christ challenges the entirety of the powers of pagan religion and culture. While it is true that he speaks of the "christening" of the powers, this is precisely *not* the same thing as taking them into a Christian civilization as is. Berkhof has completed very careful historical studies of the age of Constantine and the nature of the compromise which that name represents, and this is not the kind of "Christianization of the powers" that he advocates.

Perhaps the best description of the impact of Christian proclamation upon the powers is that they are sobered or made modest. What had been treated as an end in itself comes to be seen as a means of furthering human welfare. What had been a source of social and cultural stability becomes part of a process of change. As long as the prior commitment of the Christian community is clear, the disarmed powers can be held in check.

It can also happen, however, that instead of accepting the news of their reduction to a modest estate, the powers might rebel or reaffirm their idolatrous independence. Berkhof speaks here of angry powers: fascism, nihilism, or other forms of secularism. Their vitality in conflict is greater than that of earlier paganism because they respond to the message of the meaningfulness of human life and history through Christ by affirming a counter-purpose just as strongly.

Therefore, in all of the challenges posed to the church, the key to its success in witness and faithfulness will be maintaining its own identity. It is the church's task to sober the powers. The church that understands its own identity may be preserved from the temptation to assign a halo to the tamed power structures. In the other cases, where the rebellious powers are again visible in their destructiveness, it will be the confessing unity of Christians that will permit them to withstand such pressures faithfully.

This is not the position taken by the mainstream Christian churches of the last two thousand years. As we have seen, whether Protestant or Catholic, the churches generally identified themselves with the power structures of their respective societies rather than seeing it as their duty to call them to modesty and resist them in their continuing rebelliousness.

The cultural unity of Christendom began to break up not because the churches saw clearly the path of biblical faithfulness but because the unity they had been leaning upon began to break apart of itself in the "Wars of Religion" ending in 1648. It was only logically possible to think of the church and society as one—of the church of Rome united with the empire of Rome—when each of these was worldwide. Although it never was really true, it was possible for both the Roman church and the Roman Empire to *claim* to be worldwide. After 1648, the several churches are obliged to accept identification with a given nation or state. This is no longer the unity of the total church with the total empire but rather of a particular provincial national church with a particular local government.[1] We may

---

1. Author's note in the text: "(Later we may even observe a further breaking up, in which a given religious body will tie itself to a particular social class or political party within a society.)"

label this situation "neo-Constantinianism," a new kind of unity of church and world in which the worldwide character of the age of Constantine is lost but the fusion of church and society is maintained. Now the church has become the handmaiden of a particular society and not of society as a whole, of a particular ruling class and not of a population as a whole.

The next logical step in the same direction in the Western world was to take place in the century of political revolutions from 1776 to 1848. During this time, a progressive secularization occurs whereby it becomes visible that one can no longer assume the identity of church and society. It may happen, as it has come to pass in North America, that formal ties between church and state are broken for political or philosophical reasons. Nevertheless, the identification of church and society remains strong in the minds of the population. Despite all its separation of church and state, the United States considers itself a Christian nation, and most citizens will attend occasional church services.

In a country like Sweden, the process of secularization went in the other direction: the churches continue to enjoy formal government support but no longer have significant popular support. As different as these two patterns are, they share the way in which they secularized the Constantinian dream. Now it is possible for the church to bless the nation—for the church and nation to support one another reciprocally—even though it is widely recognized that one can no longer speak of society as a specifically Christian one. In the United States, in spite of separation of church and state, the military and the political loyalties of Christians are witness to the deep moral and emotional identifications that still obtain. In a place like Scandinavia, the church continues to support national policy and the government continues to support the clergy regardless of the presence or absence of convinced Christian individuals or congregations. For this stage, where the church blesses the society (a specific national society) without formal unification or without religious strength in that society, we may use the artificial label "neo-neo-Constantinianism." The unity of church and world is two steps removed and yet the church is still morally subservient.

There is yet one more step that can be taken in the evolution of the church-state symbiosis. In our century, secular philosophies can develop and come to power which are not only separate from the church but, in fact, opposed to the religious side of culture. We find society being led by secularists—perhaps anti-religious or at least post-religious—and convinced that secular values are best understood and attained without religious sponsorship. Even here, where society is ready to disavow religion, it is possible for the church to try to maintain her position by arguing that the process of secularization can also be carried on in the name of the church. Some current Protestant thought in East Germany and Czechoslovakia understands the "non-religious interpretation of the biblical message" proposed by Dietrich Bonhoeffer as a way of clearing the decks for the mutual recognition of Protestant Christianity and Communist government. In the West, a similar transposition of the gospel in terms of non-religious secular language is being proposed as the price of relevance for the message of the church in this world. In the younger nations, concerned with overcoming the restricting influence of earlier generations, Christians strongly argue their ability and obligation to make common cause with the secular governments under which they live, preferring this secular identification to a religious one. The concern of the church to be allied with a post-religious secularism, as long as it is popular, can perhaps be called "neo-neo-neo-Constantinianism."

All of these efforts to plead the case of the church before the bar of secular analysis have in common a version of one starting assumption: it is what happens that really matters, the real frame of salvation is in the world and not in the church, what God is really doing is being done for all of society and not in the Christian congregation. Secondly, it is assumed that if "we" help by doing our share, it will be possible to assure the world about the fulfillment of the salvation which is already in the process of manifesting itself. Therefore, we will do well to ally ourselves with whatever powers are at hand as a way to share in the creation of a society worthy of humanity.

Our first assignment cannot be to criticize any one of these positions but to note what they have in common which permits grouping them under the same heading in spite of far-reaching differences. All of these Constantinian postures will limit the validity of the church, of the New Testament, or of Jesus Christ as a source of ultimate standards because the framework of social development in this world is itself already a revelation, a norm of its own. In the beginning, this secular revelation came through the power of the Roman Emperor himself; in contemporary secularism, the revelation comes through the capacity of society and its technocrats that work to make things come out right. This other truth, i.e., the survival and prosperity of the national unit, has become more determining than the biblical imperatives. In this connection, the church is seen, primarily, neither as a gathered congregation of believers nor as a critic of official policy but rather as chaplain to society, providing resources to meet specifically spiritual needs.

Another common trait of all of these kinds of the Constantinian view is that the church always identifies with "our side." It was the churches of the West that supported the United Nations' action in Korea; it is the churches of the socialist countries that assume the superior value of Marxist secular society. The church *never* identifies with "the other side."

At each level, there is a strong desire to reject the previous "marriage." In the sixteenth century, one might have argued that it was wrong for the church to be allied with Constantine. Therefore, in order to break up the Holy Roman Empire, we had to ally the church with national governments. Next, one might have argued that it was wrong to identify the church with national governments so we had to establish our identity with a select class in society. Or it was wrong to link church organization with the state, so we had to let the church proclaim that the proper Christian form of government is the one in which church and state are separate but allied. Later, it was wrong for the church to be allied with Western liberal humanism, so we had to let it make an alliance with the Marxist democratic republics. Thus, over and over again, the present alliance of the church with the world is explained as necessary to overcome the previous one. What is rejected is not the *principle* of the church's subservience to the secular order but only her wrong judgment in staying with an obsolete ally.

Simply from the perspective of logic, one would need to ask whether three successive changes of alliance do not make it appear wrong that the liaison was accepted in the first place. The church has tried to strengthen its hold on society and its usefulness within society at each of these stages by taking the side of the persons of the ideologies currently in power. Then, when a given ruler or ideology needs to be rejected, the church would take the side of the next triumphant one. As it has worked out, however, the succession has not brought progress but disillusionment. Therefore, we should ask whether the mistake of the church in earlier days was not that it allied itself with the wrong power—with the outgoing ruler rather than the incoming one—but that she accepted the principle of sanctifying a given social order at all. Should we not question the church's readiness to establish a symbiotic relationship with every social structure rather than questioning only the tactics of having allied itself with the wrong one?

That is the question that we would have to ask from the perspective of logic. Assuming that the church desires to find a strong position within society and to make a solid impact, would it not do better to refrain from alliances with the powers that be? Our concern, however, should not be the logical question but the theological one. Does the gospel give us guidance about how to avoid unwholesome alliances? Should we not expect to find that the contribution of the Christian church would be both most faithful and most effective where it maintains its separate identity from the rebellious powers?

As a matter of fact, this is what we do find in historical study: the church has been most successful in contributing wholesomely to the growth of a society and to the welfare of humanity when it has precisely avoided alliance with the dominant political or cultural power. Similarly, if the church is to make a contribution worthy of the church in the years to come, it must not look for the obvious pattern of "what is going on in the world" in order to join the movement with the claim, "It is God that is doing this!" Not everything that is going on is the action of God. Rather than ask, "What is God doing in the world?" should it not rather ask, "How do we discern where and how God is acting in all that which is going on in the world?" The answer to this question will not be provided by reading the surface of day-to-day history but by the Spirit-led insight of a discerning community. We will not say, as people in our day with a deep sense of human needs are prone to say, "Revolution is the will of God" and leave it at that. We shall rather learn to ask, "In a world where revolution is popular and probable, what is the form of the revolutionary servanthood to which we are called?" Whether in the ancient society or the future one, our call is not to be master but slave. Therefore, what the church needs to discern is not how to establish the most promising alliance with the most constructive powers currently at work in society but how to retain moral independence of such forces in order to exercise a ministry toward them that only it can exercise, namely, a constant call to sobriety and respect for human dignity.

Instead of Efficacy

I have argued repeatedly that the link between our obedience and expected results must be broken. If we were to justify our behavior on the basis of its promised social effect, this would drive us into pride and the abuse of power at those points where we achieve the goals we set and into resignation and withdrawal at those points where we are unable to dominate. In either case, we are lured away from the purity of our servanthood. We cannot "sight down the line" of our obedience toward the attainment of the goals for which we hope.

What then are the value and the relevance of our hope? What is the reason for our obedience? What is the rationale for our being actively present in a world which we cannot control? If we cannot guarantee bringing about the desired ends, what is the continuing reason for concern?

> *Therefore, since we are surrounded by so great a cloud of witnesses, let us also lay aside every weight and the sin that clings so closely, and let us run with perseverance the race that is set before us, looking to Jesus the pioneer and perfecter of our faith, who for the sake of the joy that was set before him endured the cross, disregarding its shame, and has taken his seat at the right hand of the throne of God.*
> *Consider him who endured such hostility against himself from sinners, so that you may not grow weary or lose heart.*[2]

The reasonableness of our continuing obedience in a world we do not control is its conformity to the work of Christ. The connection between our obedience and the ultimate attainment of desirable ends is analogous to the hidden lordship of the crucified one and the risen Lord.

1. There is the relevance of the *sign*. When Jesus washed his disciples' feet, he made no lasting contribution toward the hygiene of Palestine. Yet this deed demonstrated a posture in the world which itself is of both spiritual and ethical validity. Likewise, when Christian concern is devoted to the care of the hopelessly ill, the mentally handicapped, or the unproductive aged, its usefulness must be measured not by any statistical index of economic usefulness but by the recognition that it individually and collectively symbolizes that an individual is here for the sake of the need of the neighbor. To cite another example, numerous dimensions of the civil rights movement in the United

2. Heb 12:1–3.

States must be understood with this symbolic kind of measurement. Such actions are not instrumental but significant. What matters about such a deed is not the changes it immediately brings about in the social order nor the shifting of reluctant persons or organizations to positions they did not want to hold, but what it *signifies*. Since we are not the Lord of history, there will be times when the only thing to say is a word, or a word enclosed in a deed, to which no one seems ready to listen and which will coerce no one. Nonetheless, this must be said in the confidence that it is our Lord and his Holy Spirit and not we and our eloquence that will make a message of our sign. This is the hope which our efforts seek to proclaim. Perhaps Christians would be well advised to ask that the demonstrations and manifestations of social protest should remain just that, that they demonstrate or manifest something rather than becoming tools of coercion and pressures to force people to bargain against their will.

2. The relevance of a transcendent hope is sometimes that of the *wonder*. Every account of major social movements (such as the North American civil rights movement) gives some attention to the dimension of the unexpected. Perhaps a discerning Christian description of history would find more such unexplainable—Christians would call them providential—coincidences at crucial turning points. Often, the brilliant solutions, the courageous resistances, and the reconciling initiatives have not been the result of strategic scheming but have been given by the situation in a way that is a surprise, a revelation, "a wonder in our eyes."[3] The planners have seen things taken out of their hands and solutions were found which would not have happened if they had remained in control. It is also so with the lordship of the crucified one. His power is not the divine rubber stamp with which he is obliged to seal our best efforts but a treasure in earthen vessels, a strength that is made perfect in weakness.

3. The relevance of the transcendent ideal is sometimes that of *unmasking idols*. There are times when a society is so sweepingly under the control of an ideology that its greatest need is for someone to find a point at which that individual will say a clear "no" on the ground of a commitment to a higher loyalty. Concerning those who refused to

---

3. See Mark 12:11.

be enrolled in Hitler's racist crusade, we have no right to say that they were practically or morally obligated to have an alternative social strategy before refusing to conform. The rejection of that idolatry is not conditioned upon our immediate ability to fabricate a substitute society. There are times, surprisingly many, when the nonconformist and the conscientious objector make creative new social discoveries. But their obligation to refuse conformity is independent of that capacity to produce good results.

4. The relevance of the transcendent hope is that of the *pioneer*. It has been argued often enough that Anglo-Saxon democracy is traced upon the outline of the congregational meeting of evangelical fellowships. It was the church which pioneered schools and hospitals in other ages, creating the institutional patterns which could later be generalized and supported by the state. In our age, it was the church service agencies that developed the concept of voluntary service for young people now being picked up by numerous Western governments in forms such as the Peace Corps. It was the Christian Committee for Service in Algeria which pioneered, in a small way, a reforestation project which gives some promise of restoring something of the agricultural wealth to North Africa which was there before the grazing habits of the goat made much of that land a desert. Christians can undertake "pilot" efforts in education and other kinds of social service because, unlike government agencies, they can afford to take the risk of failure.

5. The relevance of a transcendent hope is that of the *spring in the desert*. If water can be found in desert country, it is because at some unknown and unseen distant place, unmeasured amounts of water soaked into the soil and were lost. Water can be found as a nearly miraculous source of sustenance in a desert only because it seeped away in some distant place over a long enough period of time to create pressure in the veins of porous rock that drove it all the way to the place of its appearance. So it is with the deeds of Christian obedience. Lost into the earth, seeping away unseen and uncounted, they contribute to the building up of pressures, creating an underground reservoir of healing and quickening power which can be drawn on at the point of a person's greatest thirst. The social scientist would

speak here about the creation of mores or the development of public opinion to raise the general level of one's capacity for unselfish behavior. These are simply other ways of affirming that the connection between my obedience and the fulfillment of God's purposes must include my losing track of my own effectiveness in the larger reservoir of loving pressures.

6. The relevance of a transcendent hope is that of the *mirage*. If we speak of the genuine mirage and not of hallucinations, what the traveler sees on the horizon, although it does not lie on the immediate horizon, is still really there and still straight ahead as the ultimate goal of her travel. The traveler will not reach that goal as soon as it seems that she should, but what she sees ahead is of the same shape and character and in the same direction as the reality of his or her ultimate destination. In the American civil rights movement, when the demonstrators sing "We're Marching on to Freedom Land" in the streets as if this were just around the corner, this is a mirage. Even the most successful outcome of the efforts to do away with racial injustice still will leave North American society with generations of repairs and rebuilding to do. Nevertheless, the effort is justified by the vision of that city set on a hill to which God will call all nations to learn the law of the Lord together in the last days and to forge their weapons of war into gardening tools. We do not pilgrimage toward the holy city because we can get there on our own power but because we want to be the kind of persons and community who will not be out of place there when God brings Jerusalem down to us from heaven.

And so, in a number of ways, the connection between our obedience and the fulfillment of God's purposes is analogous to: finding life through the cross, finding power through weakness, finding wisdom through foolishness, finding wealth by casting one's bread on the waters, and finding sisters and brothers and houses and lands by forsaking the same. In short, we save life by losing it. This is the gospel pattern of social significance. The last and deepest reason for considering Christ and not democracy or justice or equality or freedom to be the hope of the world is not the negative consideration that these kinds of hope will ultimately be incomplete or disappointing (which is true) or that they may lead those devoted to them to fall into pride and brutality for their sake. The ultimate limitation of these hopes is that in their search to be strong and in their urge to provide justice, they are not yet powerful enough. They locate humanity's worst need in the wrong place: outside itself. *"For the weapons of our warfare are not merely human, but they have divine power."*[4] Those for whom Jesus Christ is the hope of the world will not measure their contemporary social involvement by its promise of effectiveness tomorrow, or by its success in providing jobs and freedom, but only by its identity with the Lord in whom they have placed their hope. *This* is why they are sure to succeed.

4. 2 Cor 10:4.

13. Revolution and Gospel

THE WORD "GOSPEL" HAS become for us a tired word. In common Roman Catholic thought, the evangelical counsels point to a more demanding level of moral choice than is required of the average believer. Gospel thus means the revealed demand for a sacrificial life. In Europe and Latin America, "evangelical" serves to designate the Protestant churches over against the Roman. In the Anglo-Saxon countries, the same term will indicate conservative theology and individual religious experience over against the "high church" and liberal theologies. Gospel is then a correctly understood body of truths or the call for a proper kind of personal Christian experience.

Therefore, we must stretch our minds if we are to become able to understand the full and powerful meaning of "good news." The Greek term for "evangel" refers not to just any kind of welcome information but to a particularly public kind of good news, the annunciation of which makes a great difference to all hearers. The announcement that a battle has been won or an heir born to the royal throne is not just news to satisfy the curiosity of the people. It has to do with their continuing liberty and prosperity, even with their existence as a people. Therefore, gospel is, in the fullest sense, the proclamation of a fact that makes a fundamental and saving difference for all who hear.

It is in this sense that the term is used in the Bible. Luke designates the announcements of John the Baptist as "evangelizing":

> Even now the ax is lying at the root of the trees; every tree therefore
> that does not bear good fruit is cut down and thrown into the fire
> ... His winnowing fork is in his hand, and he will clear his threshing

floor and will gather his wheat into the granary; but the chaff he will
burn with unquenchable fire.[1]

This was an announcement with obvious economic implications. The multitudes asked, "*What then shall we do?*" He answered, "*Whoever has two coats must share with anyone who has none; and whoever has food must do likewise.*"[2]

The first usage of the term by Jesus as reported by Luke was in his quotation from the book of Isaiah: "*The Spirit of the Lord is upon me, because he has anointed me to bring* good news *to the poor.*"[3] This announcement is likewise a proclamation of radical and rapid social change: "*He has sent me to proclaim release to the captives and recovery of sight to the blind, to let the oppressed go free.*"[4] Thus, to the first hearers of Jesus as to those of John the Baptist, the expectation they awakened was one of a new order of things which they announced as being "at hand."

Modern Gospels

If we cast about in modern language for terms which find the same echo in the hearts of the poor as Jesus' announcement of the kingdom did, the language would be that of revolution, independence, or liberation. In our day, these are the names under which war and violence are justified. Great masses of people are ready to agree that the social system under which they have lived in the past must change. They no longer are willing to be told that their ancient system enjoys divine sanction or that those now governing them can be trusted.

So it seems—the Western liberal, the militaristic, and the Marxist ideal of revolution agree—that *revolution* is the only answer. Those in power must be replaced, by violence if necessary—and it is always necessary—for the sake of the better order which can only come if they cease to govern. Some would even say that the better order is sure to come if this group of oppressors can be removed.

There is a dangerous confusion and oversimplification in the modern glorification of revolution and of the war of liberation. This is already

1. Matt 3:10–12.
2. Luke 3:10–11.
3. See Luke 4:18 and Isa 61:1. Emphasis added by author.
4. Ibid.

observed in the fact that widely conflicting kinds of organizations, from the communist guerrilla to the fascist junta, can use almost identical words for their rise to power. We shall see more of this later. For now, the point is simply to sense the appropriateness of our contemporary mentality as a frame for understanding what the "revolutionary" message of Jesus must have meant to the people of his time.

In other ages, individuals have been deeply concerned with a sense of personal guilt. For them, the primary meaning of the gospel had to do with how one can be justified before God, how one can be assured of the mercy of one's Creator and Judge. In still another age, people were preoccupied with mortality, with the temporary and precarious character of life. In that context, the central concern in understanding the work of Jesus Christ was how he brings immortality to human beings. But in our century, as in the age of Jesus, the problem that exercises people of good will is the problem of injustice. Here is where it hurts. We need a gospel to speak to this.

Nowhere is this deep social concern more surprisingly but more clearly portrayed then in the *Magnificat*, that hymn of the hope of the Galilean maiden Mary:

> *He has shown strength with his arm;*
> *he has scattered the proud in the thoughts of their hearts.*
> *He has brought down the powerful from their thrones,*
> *and lifted up the lowly;*
> *he has filled the hungry with good things,*
> *and sent the rich away empty.*[5]

The Available Choices

In Palestine in the years of Jesus' silent preparation for public ministry, it is easy to see what the possible avenues were. The lines were clearly drawn. There was no middle ground. In the face of Roman domination, one had to choose:

1. On one hand, there was the strategy of the Herodians, the Sadducees, and the publicans. Their decision was to make the most of a

---

5. Luke 1:51–53.

minimum alliance with the powers in control while attempting to preserve the core of the faith of the fathers while keeping the worship practices going.

2. Or, at the other extreme, there was the path of the Maccabees and the Zealots. Directly attacking the oppressor—with his own weapons of military violence and more immediately concerned with destroying the tyrant than informed about how to keep order if they should be successful—wave after wave of revolutionary freedom fighters had already broken on the rocks of Roman power by the time of Jesus. But in every generation there were earnest patriots who again could hope that God would bless the next insurrection waged in his name with success. That such a choice was a serious possibility for Jesus himself is clear from the gospel story if we give careful attention to the nature of his temptations, the content of his preaching, the social backgrounds of his disciples, the expectation of the crowds who heard him so eagerly, and his capture in the garden.

3. There was a third option: complete withdrawal. One could leave it to God to tolerate or to judge the corrupt Jewish and Gentile orders which one could not change. Gathering in the desert, individuals could devote themselves to the study of scriptures and to the rigorous observance of the law in all its purity while awaiting the miracle of redemption. We know that this was one of the open possibilities as well. Jesus could have joined one of the desert monasteries around the Dead Sea.

It takes little imagination to note how similar these three options are to the choice before Christians in our day: conservation, revolution, or withdrawal. As in his day, the reasons which lead sincere persons to choose one or the other are obvious. The guidance of those who tell us that these are the only choices is just as insistent now as then. But this is a choice Jesus refused to make. He did not join the Sadducees nor the Qumran sect. But, neither was he a Zealot. He proclaimed a new order, a kingdom, but rejected violence as a way to bring it into being.

Our purpose is to ask how Jesus' good news relates to our revolutionary hopes. Jesus described all human sovereignty in his last instructions to his disciples around the table of the Last Supper:

> *The kings of the Gentiles lord it over them; and those in authority over them are called benefactors. But not so with you; rather the greatest among you must become like the youngest, and the leader like one who serves.*[6]

The exercise of lordship over others, he says, is typical of "the nations," of the order of things from which he has come to free people. He does not approve of this fact as a divine institution (as the conservative religious position would) nor does he reject it as if it is wrong or it could be essentially otherwise (as would the revolutionary). It just is the case that humans rule over humans. There is no society where this does not obtain. Those who seek to change the fact can do so only by confirming its truth in an effort to take the rule themselves.

It is the case that "they let themselves be called benefactors." It is of the nature of human sovereignty to make a moral claim for itself. This claim has an element of truth about it and—as Jesus' phrasing hints half-ironically—an element of self-glorifying exaggeration.

This piercing description of political reality points us to the common aspect of both conservatism and rebellion. Each exercises lordship. Each claims to be doing so for the benefit of its subjects. The subjects are the same. The character of lordship is the same as well. Only the rulers and their ideologies change. Rulers and revolutionaries are more alike than they are different. The ruler claims to keep order at the cost of regimentation or injustice. The revolutionary promises a new order but all he can deliver is a new regime and a different selection of injustices.

What is morally lacking in the political revolutions of our day is not that they are too radical but that morally they are too much like the movements they oppose. They would overcome dictatorship with dictatorship, military regimentation with military regimentation. Jesus does not say it can be otherwise . . . among the Gentiles. But his description warns us against the modern myth of armed revolt as a sure way to achieve a better society. Yet Jesus' rejection of Maccabean revolution is not based on pessimistic practical predictions or on the knowledge of how alike all revolutions are whatever the flag they fly, but on his own calling: "*But I am among you as one who serves.*"[7] The nearly parallel text from Matthew's Gospel is even more explicit: "*And whoever wishes to be first among you*

6. Luke 22:25–26.
7. Luke 22:27.

must be your slave; just as the Son of Man came not to be served but to serve, and to give his life a ransom for many."[8] The reason it is not the business of Jesus' disciples to rule over others is that when he came to save humanity, the pattern of his combat with evil was one of service and suffering. We are to do likewise. This proposes a genuine social revolution, a revolution so radical that it is not satisfied with limiting itself to changing the definition of ultimate goals to be reached by the application of the same methods of power used by the oppressors, a revolution so radical that it begins with a new set of methods. Jesus does not defend the status quo either explicitly or by withdrawal, nor does he spiritually succumb to it by agreeing that the only way to defeat it is with its own weapons of violence. Jesus begins by teaching and practicing a different kind of life in the midst of the world that can respond to such perfect love only with hate.

The Paradox of Gospel Ethics

We shall return to the question of revolutionary effectiveness. First, however, we must look at the reasons which have kept Christians over the centuries from seeing Jesus as the judge and redeemer of social relationships. Perhaps these objections can best be described in the forms they have taken in recent Protestant thought.

1. First of all, it is said that we must choose between the Jesus of history and the Jesus of dogma.

    If Jesus is the divine Word incarnate, then what we are concerned about is the metaphysical transaction whereby he entered into humanity for our salvation. We can then leap, as does the creed, from his manger to the cross. His teachings and his social involvement will be neither very interesting nor very binding for us because that is not what salvation is about.

    Or, on the other hand, we must seek to understand "the Jesus of history" in his human context, as this can be described by careful historical study. We shall then find a man like any other human, a reforming rabbi, an understandable product of the society that brought him forth—sometimes mistaken—and who will have for us only such authority as we agree to ascribe to him. Protestant research in the nineteenth century chose the Jesus of history until

8. Matt 20:27–28.

Albert Schweitzer demonstrated that Jesus "as he really was" really did take himself for some kind of messiah and think that his time represented the end of history. Then Protestant thought turned again to metaphysics, using historical and literary criticism not to discover Jesus but to find how the gospel documents project the understanding that the early church had of itself. This understanding, like the earlier concern for incarnation, was attached to Jesus' name but not to the details of his human career or teaching.

The gospel texts refuse to permit us such a choice. For them, the Jesus of history is the Jesus of faith. In listening to the reforming rabbi, we understand the existential obedience demanded of the church. If we observe the messianic Jesus Schweitzer rediscovered more closely, we find a description of the gospel revolution which is utterly precise and practicable, because in him the kingdom indeed has come.

2. Traditional Protestant analysis has demanded a choice between the prophetic and the institutional.

On the one hand, the prophet condemns us and crushes us under his demand for perfection. Ultimately, he is right both (a) in convicting us of our sin by contrast with the perfection of the law and (b) in pointing us to the ideal that our feeble efforts intend but are without immediate import as far as today's society—and the society we shall have to manage tomorrow—is concerned. With love, self-sacrifice, and nonviolence, one cannot assume responsibility for the world. Depending only on the grace of God, one cannot act in history.

On the other hand, those who are called to be concerned for the survival and the management of institutions will have to accept violence in order to reduce it. They will accept inequality and exploitation in order to eliminate them one day. They will use dictatorship to work toward the withering away of the state. This kind of service is imperfect and modest enough but necessary in order to avoid something worse. While respecting the prophet, most of us will choose to serve the institution.

If we reflect on Jesus' proclamation of the kingdom and its character faithfully, we must refuse this choice. The kingdom that Jesus said was at hand—the new ordering of things in which violence, the oath, and adultery would have no place and in which the liberation of the captives and the enunciation and the proclamation of good news to the poor have pride of place—did not represent the end of all time without connection to yesterday or tomorrow. What Jesus proposed was a new way of acting, a new way of enacting the Jubilee, an institution whose application within history would have certain precise, limited, practicable effects. This becomes especially clear if we accept the genial hypothesis of Andre Trocmé that Jesus intended, literally, to announce a year of Jubilee. But the same logic applies even without this hypothesis. Jesus did not radically suspend historical continuity in any of his teaching. He simply called for forgiveness and a new beginning.

3. The habits of Protestant moral thought demand that we choose between the apocalyptic kingdom and the inner kingdom.

On the one hand, we may understand Jesus as announcing an immediate and complete end of history, an event that was to take place tomorrow or at least soon after his death. The apostles maintained this expectation for a generation but finally had to admit that he had been mistaken about the date.

The other interpretation is that he must have been speaking only of an internal kingdom since Jesus could not be in error. He spoke of such a kingdom and its coming only in order to teach, in the language of the time, about an inner, spiritual order whose reality remains hidden to the unbeliever and to the historian.

But once again, the gospel accounts will not suffer such a dilemma. The kingdom of God is a social and not an invisible order. But it is not a universal upheaval independent of the will of humans. It is an order of concrete loving and forgiving obedience which people need only to accept, a real possibility of a new order that is announced for today and, allying grace and justice, is open to whomever will accept. People refused that promise, rejecting the kingdom which had drawn near to them. But Jesus predicted that as well, and he was not mistaken.

When the thought of our age would ask us to choose between the respect for the individual and the movement of history, Jesus tells us that the neighbor, the concrete individual with whom we have to do at the moment, *is* the meaning of history. Told that we must choose between absolute love which is always crucified and efficacy which is always violent, we who confess a resurrected Lord and have observed how ineffective the power of the sword is for anything but destructive purposes shall refuse to choose.

The Gospel for Secular Humanity

If it can be argued that traditional Protestant moral explanations do not do away with the force of the demands and the promises of Jesus, are we not left with a far greater challenge in the demands of the poor for justice? Whatever Jesus said, we must still face the question of those who have opened their ears to the cries of the poor. After all, does there not come a time when the only possible hope is violent revolution? Are there not times when the limited violence intended in the revolution can be "a paradoxical expression of love" (the phrase is from one of the sectional reports of the 1961 Christian Peace Conference)?

We readily grant that those who resort to the use of violence sincerely intend to keep it within limits. Yet history can show us no significant cases where it has been possible to hold such violence to the intended modest limits. Likewise, we can grant the sincerity of those who believe that their resort to arms is an expression of benevolent intentions or of love. This is the profession of every despot. Why should it not be the intention of more idealistic people that the violence they exercise might be for the sake of the common good? But under the test of time it does not happen to be the case that any military or revolutionary violence can thus serve human welfare. At most, this could be said—and even then only under strict limitations—of that particularly ordered kind of power which is exercised by the police in times of peace. The sword cannot serve the common good for the simple reason that the one against whom it is used is also part of the human community. The elimination of the oppressor by someone more violent, which is necessary if the effort is to succeed, cannot end oppression. The only way to destroy one's enemies, in the language of Abraham Lincoln, is to make them one's friends. The only radical cure to human conflicts (literally, the only cure which reaches the root of the evil) is reconciliation.

The great moral power of nonviolence as a tool of social change does not come from any self-righteousness that would claim that the purity of noninvolvement is either a possible or a worthy goal. The radical character of Jesus' type of revolution stems from (a) its recognition of where an individual's deepest social need truly lies, namely, in the hatred which corrupts even the best of ideals, institutions, and reforming intentions, and (b) its deeper view of the human community in which the offender and the oppressed are included.

When we state that the deepest need of an individual lies in that kind of hateful self-centeredness which corrupts the intentions of the user of power, two very profound misunderstandings lie close at hand, misunderstandings which have found abundant effect in both Protestant and Catholic circles and which are currently widely denounced in ecumenical circles under the (historically not quite correct) label of pietism.

One side of this regrettable argument would be the conclusion that since an individual is a sinner and efforts toward social betterment are not free from sinfulness, we should do nothing to attempt to change the face of society. We should, following the pattern which was one of Jesus' options, i.e., withdraw—whether geographically or spiritually—from the arena of social conflict in order to keep ourselves safe from risks and contamination. The other line of argument begins with other assumptions but will have the same effect of not deeply changing things. Recognizing that certain persons wield great power in society, this strategy—applied by the movement of Moral Rearmament among others—will be especially concerned to find these powerful persons, to respect them in order to change their attitude, and then to expect them not to renounce their power but use it in a more helpful way.

This misunderstanding of the pattern of Jesus' ministry can be clearly avoided by recognizing that the rebellion and unfaithfulness against which he warned his disciples is not adequately understood either as the infringement of certain rules which we can avoid by noninvolvement nor by a purely inward disposition which could be changed by conversion while one retains his former wealth and power. We observe with great clarity that a quite different pattern is being drawn whether we look at the words of Jesus, at his own earthly ministry among needy men and women in a very tense social situation, or at the pattern of life which he and his apostles commended to the young church. This is not a withdrawal from concern for secular society nor is it a new ideology to justify the seizing of power by a revolutionary Christian minority. It is a new conception of the nature of Christian presence in the everyday world.

The Way of the Cross in Social Change

Jesus' pattern of ministry begins with *identification*. "He became poor for us"[9] is a symbolic statement but also a literally true one. The renunciation of wealth for himself and the insertion of the divine life into the humblest segments of society (from birth to death), represents a far more radical reorientation of values than we have seen in our generation among any of those who expect their retreat into exile or into the underground to be followed rapidly by a rise to power and its material rewards.

Jesus' *renunciation of efficacy* was still more profound in its implication for the character of moral decision. The glorification of and the trust in the power of power is the first point where all three of the previously discussed options agree. Conservatives would use power because they believe it is effective to maintain peace and order. Revolutionaries would use the same kind of power because they believe it is effective in attaining a better kind of peace or order. Quietists withdraw from the scene either because they see that no kind of desirable peace and order can be obtained or because they believe it can be obtained but would require the use of methods that would not be right. All three parties share the fundamental understanding that decisions are made on the basis of the likelihood of attaining desirable goals by the use of appropriate methods.

Jesus, however, renounces not only violence but the concern for efficacy that justifies violence. According to the pattern so beautifully stated later by Francis of Assisi, it is those who lose their lives who gain it, those who renounce houses and lands who find them again even in this world, those who die who are resurrected to eternal life.[10] Therefore, the thread connecting faithfulness and effectiveness is cut. We no longer justify, on the basis of results, action which we could not justify as an expression of person love. Even nonviolent methods of social action become questionable if they are measured strategically by their promise of producing the desired results rather than by their aptness as reflections of reconciling concern for the adversary. Violence is to be rejected, therefore, not simply

9. See 2 Cor 8:9.
10. Luke 17:33.

because it hurts someone, because it is usually inefficient in the long run, because it is hard to control, nor because it is spiritually bad for the person (although all of this is true). Fundamentally, violence is rejected because the concern for efficacy that leads to it is itself a revolt against the sovereignty of him who reigns from the tree.

A further unique characteristic of the social method of Jesus is the absolute *renunciation of deceit*. We see it in his rejection of the oath as a technique whereby falsehood could be given a place of refuge and as an immodest claim that veracity is within our ability to produce. We observe this unveiling of deceit in the tone of light irony with which Jesus reminds us that tyrants "call themselves benefactors." In the successful efforts at social change without violence on one hand and in the experience of violent social change on the other, the correlation of deceit with violence and of truth-telling with reconciliation is complete.

We have noted that the unique characteristic of Jesus' social approach is his *loving concern for the adversary*. Far from dealing with the other as the one who must be eliminated or made powerless, the adversary becomes an object of special reconciling concern. We want to stop that individual from doing evil not so much because we suffer under the evil—for that suffering we are willing to endure—but because of the harm that is self-inflicted. It is the adversary with whom we are ready to go a second mile, to whom we turn the other cheek. We are not to love the enemy simply because we love everyone and make no exceptions. (This Jesus also says.) We are to love the enemy because it is the enemy for whom God suffers the most. This is the pattern of atonement; this is also the pattern of wholesome social change.

It has been said before, but needs to be accentuated, that Christian social faithfulness begins by *refusal to cooperate* in evil institutions. This is where the readiness to suffer is first tested. This noncooperation in its purest form is not meant as a subtle form of pressure, although the boycott and the strike can become that. It is not properly chosen as a way to bring suffering upon oneself or to call public attention to an issue, though that may happen as well. It is not chosen primarily out of concern for complete moral purity because, if this were the central goal, it could more fully be achieved by emigration. The central concern behind noncooperation is that it presents the concrete test of our commitment to the new rather than to the old, to the loving rather than the selfish, to the kingdom already in our reach in which disciples are called to live. "*We must obey God rather than any human authority*"[11] is not Pharisaic self-righteousness. It is commitment to the new history of redemptive community instead of acquiescence to the self-centeredness of the world in which we have been living.

Most fundamentally of all, Jesus' strategy for change began and ended with the creation of a *covenant community*. Jesus would have been far less frightening both to the rabbis and to the Romans, and his movement would have been doomed to extinction, if it had not been for the small band and the large crowds of those who gathered around his work and committed themselves to his purposes. The creation of the covenant community is most revolutionary not simply because of technical considerations like the value of team organization, the capacity of a network of "cells" to operate clandestinely, or the opportunities that group organizations can provide for practice in self-discipline and social techniques. All of this is most important, especially if we are to be self-conscious about techniques of social change. But the most profound reason why the Christian community represents a revolutionary power is the reason to which New Testament writers point with the use of terms like "earnest" and "firstfruits": the Christian community, in all its weakness, is a demonstration of the reality of a kind of life in reconciliation, already sustained and beginning to be changed by faith, hope, and love, those three realities that abide. Therefore, it may rightly be said that the most fundamental social revolution of all time was that of Pentecost. The most urgent and ultimately the most effective task for the church in our day with its missionary responsibility in a world of rapid social change is to be the church, to discover—within the ranks of those who have let themselves be counted as the disciples of a suffering servant—that reality of new creation, of the constraining love of Christ by virtue of which "*if anyone is in Christ, there is a new creation.*"[12]

11. Acts 5:29.
12. 2 Cor 5:17.

14. The Meaning of Our ·Revolutionary Age

We have observed the revolutionary impact of the proclamation of Jesus and his disciples, the proclamation of the coming of a kingdom within the reach of humanity. But we have also seen the church's errors in attempting to administer the world for the sake of what they took to be the cause of the gospel. There seems to be growing readiness to agree that the churches have been wrong when they accepted marriage with an old social order and its authorities. In our discussion, we have suggested that it is not necessarily much better for the church to side with what it thinks is the expected or new order because the undermining of its moral independence is no different.

Yet we cannot call on the church to withdraw from the social struggle. This is not a possibility in the modern world, and, if it were possible, it would not be a better alternative. Even the effort to withdraw is of course also a taking of sides. In effect, it amounts to acceptance of the existing order.

What then is the link between the kingdom of God and the kingdoms of the world if they can neither be identical nor separate? Is this a question to be answered only by the acceptance of a mystery, the recognition that we cannot speak? Or should we, by saying that no clear answer can be given, simply open the doors for the whims of passing enthusiasm and pressures? Or is there a discernable linkage, one that would not fall into the pitfalls of either pietism or Constantinianism? And if there is such a visible connection, is it something we can only discern after the fact so that we can say of a given historical development that "God had his hand in this," or can it provide guidance as we make decisions about the future as well?

On the one hand, we want to avoid the clericalist error: our faith tells us exactly what to do and, in fact, authorizes us to use whatever means are necessary to make sure that it will happen. We must avoid this because we have seen that hunger for power is not sanctified but is rather aggravated when linked with claims to superior righteousness. On the other hand, it is not enough to say that our faith sends us out into the world, with our conscience purged and our love rekindled, to do the best we can without any substantial guidance about details.

Salvation History and World History

In recent years, students of the history of broad cultural ideas have taught us to observe a very profound connection between biblical commentary and contemporary world events, between biblical history and modern history. If there is such a connection, it may well assist us with our present search for the nature of the church's social contribution.

The modern age is characterized by both the technological revolution we refer to as the combined impact of industrialization and the development of modern science. The development of modern science is not merely an effort to understand physical nature but also the effort to provide tools for unprecedented progress in saving human life and producing cultural goods and, beyond that, the effort to create what is now called "a scientific worldview" which answers not only questions about physical nature but questions of philosophy as well.

Under the heading "social revolution," we may gather together in a similarly broad way such intellectual and cultural developments as the concept of the dignity of common humanity, the immorality of tyranny, the vision of democratic society as most worthy of humanity, and the awareness that economic considerations are a profoundly powerful force in the making of humanity and society.

At first glance, there would seem to be no immediate connection between the developments of the last two centuries of cultural history and Christian faith. Most of these developments are recent and have contributed to the weakening of a religious culture that prevailed before. They have often been propagated by persons and movements that were directly anti-religious. They seem to have arisen especially in the Christian world—and in fact to a considerable extent in the Protestant part of that world—and they represent a revolt against religion and not its outworking. But before being satisfied with this self-evident conclusion, let us look once again at what lies behind or beneath these characteristic currents of modern time.

"For you know the generous act of our Lord Jesus Christ, that though he was rich, yet for your sakes he became poor, so that by his poverty you might become rich."[1]

The thought of God's self-emptying is one of the keys to understanding apostolic thought. But it is not just a thought. The self-emptying of God is an event—at least so we confess. And if it is an event, then it is the most revolutionary event (and by that same token, the most revolutionary idea) in the history of the race. That God became *poor*, that God elected poverty as his mode of redemptive working among people is the turning point in human history—that is, if it is true as Christians confess.

"A wandering Aramean was my ancestor,"[2] said one of the earliest confessions of the Israelite faith. God's people are wanderers:

1. Abraham the nomad;

2. Joseph and his immigrant brothers;

3. Moses, the chief of a refugee caravan;

4. Jesus—born on a trip and then exiled in Egypt—who as a rabbi had no home and was outside the gate when they put him to death;

5. the polyglot profusion of Pentecost;

6. the life of the young church that could be called *"the twelve tribes in the Dispersion."*[3]

God's people are by definition homeless.

Those cultural movements that have spread the same civilization around the world and that make "one world" today our common cultural home have come, through a long process to be sure, from this relativizing of local social loyalties. The line is not short or straight. But there is a

---

1. 2 Cor 8:9.

2. Deut 26:5.

3. Jas 1:1.

line from Abraham's leaving Chaldea to our age's rejection of racial and cultural pride and provincialism.

Abraham was a layperson as well. When he left Chaldea, he left the home of the most highly developed priestly, sacramental, and superstitious view of the world. Abraham did not reject religion (seen in its ceremonial aspect) but he moved it out of the center of his preoccupations. When he needed a priest he could turn to the pagan Melchizedek, as Moses later could leave the cultic concern to his brother and his father-in-law.

This process of desacralization, culminating in Jesus' fulfillment and abolition of the priesthood, pointed forward to what we now speak of as the secular worldview and of the scientific method. Nature—and even society—is no longer explained in terms of enchantment and mystery today but is open to be studied, understood, and even managed by humanity's responsible intelligence. These are but two specimens: the rootage of modern cosmopolitanism in the itinerant freedom of the covenant people and of modern secularism in the biblical demythologizing of religious ceremony. A similar line takes its point of departure from the biblical respect for the dignity of creative work. Adam had a garden to cultivate. Micah and Isaiah tell us that everyone will have a vine and a fig tree to tend in the coming day when Jerusalem shall be reestablished as the center of the world. The line runs on from there through the Benedictines and Puritans to modernity's almost limitless respect for material efficiency.

The healing of the body was part of the core definition of his ministry that Jesus pointed to whenever he was challenged. From this definition of illness as something that ought not to be and as one of the enemies of God, a rather straight line again runs through the medical Orders of the late Middle Ages and the missionary hospitals of the last century to the population explosion of our age. Every society has its medicine men and women and even a kind of medical science, but the medical *profession* and the healing *community* were created in the Christian West as rather immediately transparent expressions of the love of Christ.

The whole Bible begins with a definition of the human person as a reflection, an image, of the divine nature. Jesus makes a moral obligation of this general descriptive statement by telling us that it is in the brother or in the needy neighbor that our love for God himself will be expressed and tested. Every civilization has some concept of the nobility of humanity, of the good human, or of the race. But it is from this conception of the individual neighbor that I encounter as a bearer of ultimate value that the Western concept of the dignity of the human person in society developed, the concept that was essential for the growth of the democratic philosophies of modern times.

The space would not suffice, nor would my competence, to argue at a greater length all of the similar lines that could be drawn: today's understanding of the person as a unit in which bodily, psychological, social, and intellectual dimensions cannot be separated; the condemnation of poverty as something that ought not to be; the ideal of a widely shared education in the background of the social group in order to enable coming generations to enter knowingly into the covenant of maturity—there would be many more.

I have already said that these lines were neither short nor straight. That they were not short is not surprising because we are dealing not with an idea but with events. It is in the nature of events that their importance can be communicated only from person to person, from place to place, and from time to time as one person deals with his or her neighbor in the light of what has happened. That atmospheric phenomenon which today we call the "sonic boom" may serve as an example. By the time we hear the thunder created by a jet airplane, the plane itself has passed far beyond the point at which it reached the speed of sound. That sound could however only reach us by mediation: one molecule of air striking another and yet another as the shock wave became an ever-widening circle, finally shaking us and our windows only after the plane is out of sight.[4] Therefore, the fact that God broke the barrier between power and poverty in the incarnation could only transform society by a similar kind of delayed impact: mediated through the expanding circles of generation after generation of persons whose dealings with their neighbors were transformed by the impact of God's presence in their midst.

Not only were the lines not short, they were not straight. Cultural historians give credit for these contemporary ideas to Karl Marx, to Freud, or to Einstein. Faithful Christians, or a faithful church, would perhaps have brought these changes sooner and more directly. But even unfaithful churches cannot keep them from happening. The only difference is that

4. Author's note in text: "(To translator: is this phenomenon something the listeners are acquainted with?)"

when it happens, it happens in spite of them under the immediate responsibility of those who reject their faith while sharing their cultural heritage.

The fact that we can discern a few fundamental biblical axioms in the distant background of the modern world and that we can also discern that the final shaping of these axioms into the building stones of modern society has been the work of rebels, does not necessarily mean that the rebels were right. Marx, Jefferson, Huxley, or Lenin—powerful as they were as creators of cultural change—were ready to attach exaggerated value to their insight and their right to change the world like the religious societies against which they rebelled. The observation that it is these rebels against official Christianity who have changed the world must drive us to ask just how this change can be understood by the church. Some would simply say that our calling is to "join the revolution," wherever it goes, with the hope that the church can help it go to the right places. We have already seen reasons for doubting that such an answer can be responsible.

What Has God Wrought?

If we are to seek to find meaning in the course of events in a biblical spirit, we must first confess that God is working a work of judgment in them. The revolutions of our day, especially when they are carried out by those who feel they are rebelling against the Christian church, are the well-earned and overdue recompense for the racism, the class identification, the overemphasis on ceremony, and the acceptance of militaristic nationalism that have characterized the official churches of the past millennium-and-a-half.

Obviously, it can be argued that the church was not as bad as its critics claim it was. We could defend the record of Christendom at some points. Not all bishops are corrupt, not all churches have trampled on the commoner, and not all of them have been racist. But we fail to understand the judgment of the course of history if we simply attempt to defend ourselves at points against the accusation that we had also committed the sins of the heathen. The deeper point of God's judgment is that we have failed to be the faithful covenant people. The official churches have not been the point at which it became visible among humans that a different kind of life had been let loose in the world.

The God who proclaims his judgment is a God of mercy. In the rebellion of the modern world against the heritage of Christendom, let us learn to welcome the calls for the church to be the church. Instead of seeking to defend an old Christian civilization and instead of trying to replace that old one with efforts to Christianize a new one, let us be freed from the oscillation between clericalism and pietism, between the stance of the "chaplain to the social order" and that of the emigrant. Let us rediscover the posture of involvement that the Bible calls servanthood which only the faith of the church can bring about and which is the only contribution for which the world needs the church.

The crises of our age have reminded us of the self-defeating character of our efforts to run our own history for our own sake. Let us take the rebelliousness of modern secular society as a call to place our trust only in him we confess as Lord. If the confession of his lordship be the language not of mere piety but of the Christian mission in the world, then our call is to renounce concern for immediate effectiveness in achieving our social ends. It is that overly great concern for social effectiveness which leads to impatience and, in turn, either to resigned withdrawal or to impatient tyranny. We should not assume that the connection between our obedience and the fulfillment of God's purposes in our society will be an instrumental connection in which we can clearly see how our deeds link up with the attainment of the goods we seek. In some crucial cases, the uniqueness of the Christian contribution in society consists in the fact that only the church can afford to fail. Only because we believe in the resurrection can we face the prospect of the cross.

The Christian contribution to the revolution of our age will be one of sobriety. As we unmask the ancient myth of the divine right of rulers, we must likewise unmask the new myth according to which a new ruler and a new social pattern will change human nature. We participate in efforts to build a better society not because those who are now in control—with their new nationalistic or humanistic or socialistic theories—are doing a good job in applying an adequate theory but because they are not. Their real need is not for a few more individuals to shore up their popularity and public acclaim but for honest and unselfish and inventive persons to give their lives in finding concrete solutions to specific needs. We best serve the social change of our age by being the least concerned for its theory and the flag it flies and the most concerned for persons and their needs.

> *Hear, you peoples, all of you;*
> *listen, O earth, and all that is in it;*
> *and let the Lord God be a witness against you,*
> *the Lord from his holy temple.*
> *For lo, the Lord is coming out of his place,*
> *and will come down and tread upon the high places of the earth.*
> *Then the mountains will melt under him*
> *and the valleys will burst open,*
> *like wax near the fire, like waters poured down a steep place.[5]*

> *By faith Abraham obeyed when he was called to set out for a place*
> *that he was to receive as an inheritance; and he set out, not knowing*
> *where he was going. By faith he stayed for a time in the land he had*
> *been promised, as in a foreign land, living in tents, as did Isaac and*
> *Jacob, who were heirs with him of the same promise. For he looked*
> *forward to the city that has foundations, whose architect and builder*
> *is God.[6]*

We spoke before of Abraham, the father of the faithful, as initiating that line that God has drawn down through human history according to which the will of God is to be done by humans. Beginning with the call of Abraham, God is no longer primarily an angry judge to be placated nor a vain monarch to be cajoled but a loving, faithful covenant partner calling people to be his fellow laborers in the building of human community.

Abraham is the father of all social revolution that is more than mere angry rebellion. Every genuinely revolutionary vision "seeks a city" that has not yet been built. Wherever we observe that pattern of thought that calls upon people to be guided by a vision of a society that is not yet, we are dealing with the spiritual heirs of Abraham.

This New Jerusalem, the vision of which strengthens the Israelite in exile, will be—if this does not press the picture too much—a society of an equalitarian economic abundance. Everyone will have a vine and fig tree. No one will be a tenant and none will be landless. Yet this economic salvation is neither described as an end in itself nor as God's first miracle. Before that peace is to be established, humans must beat their swords into plowshares and their spears into pruning hooks. Before that, they must come to Jerusalem to learn the law of the Lord. And before that—first of all—the city of God must be raised up for all to see so that they might be

5. Mic 1:2–4.
6. Heb 11:8–10.

drawn to it. The raising up of that first great city of God is not the work of a Nehemiah—with trowel in one hand and sword in the other—rebuilding the ramparts to keep his people separate. The New Jerusalem comes down from heaven.

The logic has not changed if we shift into the modern idiom. Humans can only learn to live in an economy of social justice if they learn, from a teacher outside themselves, a law according to which their weapons of war must be traded for tools of peaceful production. Whether the war of which we speak is between nations or between classes, people will not learn to share until it ends, and it will not end until they have been taught. This moral and technical learning will only be possible if people gather around an existing community of love where it is already true—not because someone figured it out as the best social strategy but as a gift of God—that it is possible to live together in love. Let it then be true, in our vision as in that of the biblical seers, that the fellowship of God's covenant people is the fountainhead of social revolution.

But God grant that we may be given the seer's vision to discern the menace of apostasy and pride as well. God's promise is not a new regime but a new society. It is precisely because the people of the promise have that hope that they can receive the gift of patience to avoid identifying God's deliverance with the coming of a new regime or with the saving of an old one.

"*So if anyone is in Christ, there is a new creation.*"[7] This is the revolution that overcomes the world. It is the concrete historical beginning of a new kind of human society as well, seedbed of all our hopes and the "down payment" of their fulfillment. There is no greater contribution that can be made by the tiny people of God in the revolution of our age than to be that people, both separate from the world and identified with its needs, both the soul of society (without which it cannot live) and its conscience (with which it cannot be at peace). We can look to the future to dream of a time when "*the home of God is among mortals*"[8] only because in the congregation of believers it is already true.

7. 2 Cor 5:17.
8. Rev 21:3.

Name Index

Name Index

Luther, Martin, 15, 73–74, 111

Martens, Paul, xvn26, xvi
Mary, 27, 60, 148
Marx, Karl, 95, 163–64
Matthew, 62
Melchizedek, 162
Meyer, Marshall, xi
Micah, 162
Míguez-Bonino, José, xi
Moses, 49, 161–62
Muntzer, Thomas, 18, 71

Nation, Mark Thiessen, x n4, xvi
Nehemiah, 167
Niebuhr, Reinhold, xiii, 73–74, 81
Nkrumah, Kwame, 94–95

Ochs, Peter, xiin11
Oldham, J. H., 131–32

Padilla, René, xii
Paul, 7–8, 23, 25–28, 38, 68, 70, 73–74,
  93, 108, 115, 121–24, 127–30,
  132
Peter, 64
Pilate, 66, 128

Pipkin, H. Wayne, 18n5
Porter, Matthew, xvn26, xvi

Roth, John D., xii

Satan, 18, 109
Savonarola, Giralomo, 111
Schweitzer, Albert, 152
Solomon, 66
Son of David, 63

Tertullian, 109
Theodosius I, 86
Toynbee, Arnold, 100
Trocmé, Andre, 61–62, 153

Valdes, Juan de, 71n19

Weber, Max, 95
Werntz, Myles, xvn26, xvi
Wesley, John, 14–15, 37
Williams, George H., 71n19

Xavier, Francis, 115

Zimmerman, Earl, xn4
Zwingli, Ulrich, 26, 30, 71, 111

Subject Index

Scripture Index